CW00661581

THE POCKET COMPANION SERIES:
COLLECT THEM ALL

The Birdwatcher's Pocket Companion
by Malcolm Tait and Olive Tayler
ISBN 978-1-862057-97-5

The Cook's Pocket Companion
by Jo Swinnerton ISBN 978-1-862057-90-6

The Fishing Pocket Companion
by Lesley Crawford ISBN 978-1-862057-92-0

The London Pocket Companion
by Jo Swinnerton ISBN 978-1-862057-94-4

The Sailing Pocket Companion
by Miles Kendall ISBN 978-1-862057-96-8

The Traveller's Pocket Companion
by Georgina Newbery and Rhiannon Guy
ISBN 978-1-862057-91-3

The Walker's Pocket Companion
by Malcolm Tait ISBN 978-1-862057-93-7

The Golfer's Pocket Companion
by Chris Martin ISBN 978-1-862058-23-1

The Literary Pocket Companion
by Emma Jones ISBN 978-1-862058-24-8

The Wildlife Pocket Companion
by by Malcolm Tait and Olive Tayler
ISBN 978-1-862058-25-5

The Gardener's Pocket Companion
by Vicky Bamforth ISBN 978-1-862057-95-1

INTRODUCTION

It can be surprisingly useful to know that England's longest parliament lasted 17 years, that the first British speeding ticket was issued to a motorist doing eight miles per hour, and that a Welshman named Captain Mainwaring invented lawn tennis. And you may one day be glad to know that five and half yards used to be called a pole, that there were 38 vineyards in England in 1086 and that tenth-century physicians cured baldness with burned bees.

For history is not just about kings, queens and battles (although much of it is, and they are in here too). It is also about the smaller things – the inventor of the bicycle, the first woman to parachute from a hot-air balloon and the possible identity of Robin Hood. It is these intriguing facts that fill all the holes in the rich fabric of our history.

So within these pages you will indeed find the Wars of the Roses, the wives of Henry VIII and the Battle of Culloden, as is right and proper. But you will also find out why Dr Crippen's head fell off, why William Cobbett hated potatoes and why 3 September 1752 never existed. And you will be reminded, once more, of the many and varied pleasures to be found in Britain's marvellous history.

Jo Swinnerton, Editor

IT WAS ONLY A JOKE

When the radio broadcast of HG Wells's *War of the Worlds* caused widespread panic in the US in 1938, because the listeners took the story of alien invasions a little too seriously, the broadcasters should not have been surprised. The BBC had achieved the same feat only 12 years before. On 16 January 1926, a piece of satire entitled *Broadcasting from the Barricades*, went out on the airwaves, prefaced with the explanation that it was a work of fiction. It then announced that a band of unemployed and angry men had run riot in London, incited to violence and vandalism by the likes of Mr Popplebury, the Secretary of the National Movement for Abolishing Theatre Queues.

Big Ben had been destroyed; the National Gallery was besieged; the Savoy Hotel had been blown up; and civil servants were being roasted alive in Trafalgar Square and hung from lampposts. For those listeners who had missed the warning at the beginning, the programme was all too real. The BBC – and the Savoy – were flooded with alarmed phone calls and the BBC was forced to apologise, although it did so with bad grace, promising that in future it would 'take no risks with its public's average standard intelligence'. It also pointed out, somewhat crossly, that had the nation truly been at risk, it would hardly have interspersed the reports of rioting with short bursts of dance music.

PAST PUZZLES

What did King John manage to hang on to in 1204?
Answer on page 145.

DAMP SQUIBS

In 1749, the Peace of Aix-la-Chapelle was celebrated with a huge fireworks display in Green Park in London. Handel composed his Music for the Royal Fireworks especially for it and rehearsals went well. But sadly the warning that a good rehearsal means a bad performance came true. The fireworks were ruined by heavy rain, although not before they had set fire to the pavilion by going off prematurely, and the evening ended with a large public brawl.

THE OLDEST CLOCK IN THE WORLD

The oldest surviving working clock in the world can be found in Salisbury Cathedral in Wiltshire. Dating from 1386, it has no face, but strikes the hours to indicate the time. It was replaced in 1884 by a new clock and languished in the tower until 1929, when it was rediscovered and put on display. It was restored to its original condition in 1956. It is estimated to have ticked more than five million times.

GREAT BRITISH FIRSTS

The first glider in the world capable of carrying a passenger was designed by Sir George Cayley in 1853. It consisted of a kite-shaped wing with a surface area of 500 square feet, and a tricycle undercarriage for the pilot. Instead of making the maiden flight himself, however, Sir George persuaded his coachman to do it for him. The coachman bravely covered about 500 yards before coming to earth with a crash, and was heard to cry out 'Please, Sir George, I wish to give notice, I was hired to drive, not to fly!' Nevertheless, he earned his place in history as the pilot of the first true aeroplane flight.

BRITISH RECORD-BREAKERS

In September 2000, the village of Denby Dale, West Yorkshire, upheld a long tradition of marking important national occasions by baking an immense meat pie. The pie weighed 12 tonnes, measured 40 feet long, nine feet wide by three feet deep, and was declared the biggest meat and potato pie in the world.

The Millennium Pie – baked to celebrate the year 2000 and the Queen Mother's 100th birthday – was the tenth in a long series of oversized Denby Dale pies. The first was baked in 1788 to celebrate the restored health of King George III, and the next to celebrate the Battle of Waterloo. The third marked the repeal of the Corn Laws and the fourth was baked to mark Queen Victoria's Jubilee in 1887. Unfortunately it was discovered that the meat was a bit off and it couldn't be eaten, so the villagers buried the offending pie in a wood and made another one. More recently a pie was baked in 1964 to celebrate four royal births in one year (to the Queen, Princess Margaret, Princess Alexandra and the Duchess of Kent).

At the ceremony for the Millennium Pie, 70-year-old former Coldstream Guard Raymond Haigh was made the Guardian of the Pie, which put him in charge of security and gave him first taste. He reported that it tasted 'beautiful'.

KING BEHAVING BADLY

In 955, officials were puzzled when the young King Edwy didn't turn up to his own coronation feast. Puzzlement turned to outrage when the 14-year-old king was discovered in his bedchamber, enjoying the company of a young lady and her mother, his new crown discarded on the floor along with the rest of his clothes.

IT'S JUST A PHASE

Fads we have endured – some of which have come back to haunt us (and some of which never went away):

Tupperware	1945
Bikinis	1946
Polyester	1953
TV dinners	1954
Hula hoops	1958
Barbie dolls	1959
Lava lamps	1964
Waterbeds	1969
Smiley logo	1960s
Bellbottoms	1960s
Mini skirts	1960s
Pet rocks	1970s
Platform shoes	1970s
Flares	1970s
Skateboards	1970s
Pong (first computer game)	1972
Star Wars	1977
Rubik's Cube	1979
Digital watches	1980s
Legwarmers	1980s
Pacman	1980s
Shell suits	1980s
Beanie babies	1990s
Tamagotchi	1997

PAST PUZZLES

Which king spent the least time in England?
Answer on page 145.

WHO WAS ROBIN HOOD?

Robin Hood is one of England's most popular legends, but historians have never been able to agree on who he might have been, or whether he existed at all. There have been many claimants to the title, but one of the more unusual of these is a 12th–century nobleman called David, Earl of Huntingdon (1152–1219).

The earliest reference to Robin Hood in English literature is in William Langland's poem *The vision of William concerning Piers Plowman*, written in 1377, in which Langland says: 'I do not know my paternoster perfectly as the priest sings it. But I know the rhymes of Robin Hood and Randolph, Earl of Chester.'

The Earl of Huntingdon was one of the leaders of the rebellion against King Henry II, which began in 1173, and one of his chief allies was Randolph, Earl of Chester. Huntingdon also later married Chester's sister, Matilda. It has often been noted that Robin Hood was not referred to as a nobleman until the sixteenth century, by playwright Anthony Munday. But while it is possible that Munday was elaborating on a romantic story, it is also likely that he was correcting a wrong done to Robin Hood in earlier Norman writings, in which the defender of the poor was portrayed as a common thief. Munday offered a further clue – in his play, Maid Marion's real name was Matilda.

Other theories have suggested that Robin Hood was a Yorkshireman, as some accounts of his life say he lived in Barnsdale, Yorkshire. But there was also a Barnsdale Wood in Rutland, much nearer to Robin Hood's traditional Nottingham. And it was owned by Huntingdon.

And there's more. Huntingdon was a close friend of Richard the Lionheart, and was one of the main supporters at his coronation. But there is no record of the Earl going on

Crusades with the King – in fact, after Richard leaves for the Holy Lands, Huntingdon disappears completely from historical record for the next four-and-a-half years. He does not re-appear until the siege of Nottingham Castle in 1194, when he is seen at King Richard's side. Huntingdon and the Earl of Chester had been besieging the castle for two days before Richard arrived to take charge, and clearly had not been on the Crusades with their King. So it is possible that Richard left the Earl behind on purpose, to wage a secret war against Prince John and keep the kingdom safe from his clutches. And it had to be a secret war; had the Earl openly defied the Prince, it could have caused war between England and Scotland. Why? Because the Earl of Huntingdon was not an English nobleman – he was the younger brother of King William II of Scotland. If this version of the legend is true, the quintessential English hero was in fact a Scot.

OLD PICTURE, NEW CAPTION

Charles realised that he had long overlooked the benefits of allowing women to join his gentleman's club.

THE KNIGHTS OF THE GARTER

In the reign of King Edward III, the King resolved to gather around him the best soldiers of Europe, in the manner of King Arthur's knights, and announced that a jousting tournament would be held on 19 January 1345, at which the knights would be selected. Edward had St George's Chapel built at Windsor and commissioned a 200-foot round table at which to seat the knights. He devised a costume bearing the image of St George tilting at a dragon, and a piece of blue ribbon that they should always wear around their necks. After the Battle of Crecy in 1346, he formalised this collection of knights as the Most Noble Order of the Garter, to which the Knights of the Garter belonged. He proclaimed that he would choose 25 of the bravest knights, and would himself be the twenty-sixth member of the order. Their motto was 'Honi soit qui mal y pense' (shame be his who thinks ill of it), supposedly the words of Edward as he tied to his leg a blue garter dropped by a lady at court. The words are written on the blue garter worn by all the knights on their left leg. Twenty-five knights are still appointed by the sovereign, and since 1987 women have also been eligible.

TAKE ONE BOILED FROG

Remedies for illnesses, from a 10th-century document

Back pain Smoke from burned goat's hair
Baldness Apply ashes of burned bees
Chilblains Treat with eggs, fennel and wine
Headache Crosswort tied to the head with a red scarf
Lack of virility Agrimony boiled in milk
Shingles A potion made from 15 types of bark
Spider bite Fried and crushed black snails

WHO WAS LORD HAW-HAW?

Just before the outbreak of World War Two, American-born William Joyce slipped out of England, where he had been studying at the London School of Economics, and headed for Germany. He had been a vociferous supporter of Oswald Mosley's fascist union, but felt so unappreciated by Mosley that he set up his own pro-Nazi organisation, called the National Socialist League. From his new home, he then made regular propaganda broadcasts in English, beginning each speech with the phrase 'Germany calling'. He developed an exaggerated public-school accent to hide his own Cockney/Irish tones and no doubt to further infuriate his listeners, which gave rise to the nickname 'Lord Haw-Haw'. Treated with derision by the English, he was tried for treason and executed after the war, as he held a British, rather than an American, passport.

A GROOVY KIND OF FAMINE

Throughout much of the Dark Ages, the poorest citizens dreaded the height of summer, as it brought the 'hungry gap', when those who could not afford to store grain, or buy food, often went hungry. They existed on a meagre diet, usually including rye bread, which was invariably mouldy. The mould that grew on it was ergot, which gave the peasants a dose of lysergic acid – otherwise known as LSD. At best, it would render them delirious; at worst, it could kill. They also scavenged in the hedgerows for poppies and hemp, which were ground up and baked in a cake. The peasants knew what this 'crazy bread' did to them, but they had little choice. The result, as contemporary historian Piers Plowman recorded, was a kind of mass hysteria expressed in over-excited summer festivals, fuelled by the unintentional drug-taking and the lightheadedness of hunger.

13

PAYMENT IN KIND

Early in the eleventh century, the King of Lombardy imposed a tax that would allow English merchants the right to trade tax-free in Pavia, Italy. It was payable once every three years, and consisted of:

- 50lb of pure silver
- Two greyhounds with gilded collars
- Two shields
- Two swords
- Two lances

The official who collected the tax also had to be paid, and his fee was two fur coats and 2lb of silver.

OVEREATERS ANONYMOUS

Gluttons whose exploits were so astonishing that they were recorded in print

John Marriott, a lawyer during the reign of James I, was the subject of a pamphlet entitled *The Great Eater of Graye's Inn, or the Life of Mr Marriott, the Cormorant*, in which he was said to have eaten a lunch prepared for 20 men.

Walter Willey was a brewer's servant celebrated for his gluttony, as proven by the November 1675 edition of the *Annual Register*, which claimed that at one meal Willey devoured a 6lb roast goose, 4lb of bread and three quarts of porter.

Nicholas Wood was a glutton of such excess that an entire book was devoted to his vice, entitled *The Great Eater of Kent, or Part of the Admirable Teeth and Stomach Exploits of Nicholas Wood*. At one meal Wood ate an entire sheep, leaving only the wool, skin, horns and bones, and on occasion he was known to eat 18lb of black pudding for breakfast.

Thomas Crapper was born in Yorkshire in 1837 and demonstrated his future work ethic by walking to London in 1848, aged 11, in search of a job. He found employment with a plumber in Chelsea, earning four shillings a week. In 1861 he set up on his own under the name of 'The Marlboro' Works of Thomas Crapper and Co'. It was a good time to be a plumber; London had just acquired its first two main sewers, which were to become 83 miles of sewers over the next four years. However, the toilets of London were still primitive structures, and Crapper set out to improve them by inventing the Water Waste Preventer, a flushing cistern that used a minimum of water to flush, had sufficient force to clean the bowl, and refilled itself effortlessly. Having perfected his invention, Crapper exhibited it at the Health Show in 1884. He proved its worth by flushing through a large quantity of 'waste', which comprised 10 apples, one sponge, some pieces of newspaper and some plumber's 'smudge' coated over the toilet pan. He went on to become sanitary engineer to royalty, receiving four royal warrants and installing the drains and bathrooms at the royal residence in Sandringham as well as in Westminster Abbey. Having found his metier, Crapper went on to design cantilevered toilets, automatically flushing cisterns and self-rising closet seats. He also designed a luxury toilet for Lily Langtry, mistress of Edward, Prince of Wales, in the form of an armchair upholstered in velvet, at a cost of £9 12s 6d. He named his toilets after London street names, which included Marlborough, Walton, Cadogan and Sloane. He died in 1910, aged 73, having left an indelible stamp on the history of the city and its cisterns.

Michael Scott was a medieval Scottish intellectual with abilities so exceptional that he was hired to tutor the Holy Roman Emperor Frederick II, and to translate for the Pope. He spoke Latin, Arabic and Hebrew and was skilled in mathematics and medicine. But it was his translation of a book called *The Secret of Secrets* that led to his reputation for less academic and more spectacular talents. Thanks to his supposed feats of magic, such as the splitting of the Eildon Hills into three peaks, he came to be known as the Borders Wizard. He was also said to have prophetic abilities, although this proved to be a mixed blessing, as he foresaw the manner of his own death. Believing that he would die from being struck on the head by a small stone, he wore a steel helmet at all times, which he took off only in church. Inevitably, it was while he was in church that a stone fell from the ceiling and hit him on the head, and he died soon afterwards. It is believed that he was buried near a cross at Melrose Abbey, along with his books of magic.

TWENTIETH-CENTURY CRISES

The Abyssinian Crisis, 1935
In October 1935, Italy invaded Abyssinia (now Ethiopia) and its ruler, Haile Selassie, appealed for help. However, Britain and France hesitated to condemn the invasion, as they were hoping to retain Mussolini as an ally against Hitler. The British and French foreign secretaries Sir Samuel Hoare and Pierre Laval instead drew up the Hoare-Laval pact, which proposed that Italy take half of Abyssinia. The pact was leaked, and a public outcry forced Hoare to resign.

ROMAN PLACE NAMES

Modern name	Roman name
England	*Albion*
Ireland	*Hibernia*
Scotland	*Caledonia*
Wales	*Cambria*
Anglesey	*Mona*
Bath	*Aquae Sulis*
Cambridge	*Granta*
Canterbury	*Durovernum*
Carlisle	*Luguvalium*
Chelmsford	*Caesaromagus*
Chichester	*Noviomagus*
Colchester	*Camulodonum*
Doncaster	*Danum*
Dorchester	*Durnovaria*
Dover	*Dubris*
Exeter	*Isca Dumnoniorum*
Gloucester	*Glevum*
Great Yarmouth	*Gernemuta Magna*
Jersey	*Caesaria*
Lancaster	*Lunecastrum*
Leicester	*Ratae*
Lincoln	*Lindum*
Liverpool	*Esmeduna*
London	*Londinium*
Manchester	*Mancunium*
Newcastle	*Pons Aelius*
Salisbury	*Sorviodunum*
Southampton	*Clausentum*
Worcester	*Vigornia*
York	*Eboracum*

SEEING STARS

In 1705, British astronomer Edmund Halley predicted that the comet seen in 1531, 1607 and 1682 would return in 1758. When it did indeed return as predicted, it was named in his honour, although Halley didn't live to see it. His calculation that it appeared every 76 years or thereabouts enabled historians to show that the comet has been recorded in literature, art and even stone tablets all the way back to 240BC. Many of its appearances have been taken as portents or omens, and it has shown up at some big moments in history. For instance:

January 66AD – The comet hovered over Jerusalem, prompting Jewish historian Josephus to write that it heralded the destruction of the city. Of course, it could be argued that his 'prophesy' helped start the Jewish Revolt of that year, which did indeed lead to the destruction of the city.

June 451 – Attila the Hun's previously invincible forces were finally beaten at the battle of Chalons by an unholy alliance of Imperial Roman and Barbarian troops. But historically it was a Pyrrhic victory. For although Attila died only two years later, the Emperor Romulus was deposed by the Barbarians in 476, effectively ending the western Roman Empire.

October 684 – The comet's appearance in the UK was followed by three months of rain, crop failure and an outbreak of plague. In other words, a typical British winter.

March 1066 – The comet appeared to Duke William of Normandy and King Harold of England. William believed it to be a good sign, and promptly invaded, defeated Harold and became King of England. For the unfortunate Harold, the comet was a very bad sign indeed.

18

June 1456 – At this point in history, the Turks were on the verge of destroying the entire Christian world. They held Constantinople, and the comet appeared just as they laid siege to Belgrade. At the time it was claimed that Pope Callistus III had excommunicated the comet, and although this is thought to be untrue, whatever he did worked – the Turks were put to flight.

20 April 1910 – The comet coincided with the death of King Edward VII. An astronomer reported that the Earth would pass through the comet's tail, which contained a poisonous gas. The fact that the amounts were so minuscule as to be completely harmless didn't stop many entrepreneurs from making a fortune selling 'comet pills', which were guaranteed to protect people. It should be noted that the people who took them did, indeed, survive unscathed. As did everyone else.

OLD PICTURE, NEW CAPTION

'Harold, the peasants are revolting.'
'I know, M'lady. Even the dogs won't eat them.'

THE COUNTIES OF 1086

The counties surveyed in the Domesday Book, in order of appearance

Kent • Sussex • Surrey • Hampshire (with the Isle of Wight) • Berkshire • Wiltshire • Dorset • Somerset Devon • Cornwall • Middlesex • Hertfordshire Buckinghamshire • Oxfordshire Gloucestershire • Worcestershire • Herefordshire Cambridgeshire • Huntingdonshire • Bedfordshire Northamptonshire • Leicestershire • Warwickshire Staffordshire • Shropshire • Cheshire (with part of Lancashire) • Derbyshire Nottinghamshire (with part of Rutland) Yorkshire • Lincolnshire

FIREFIGHTING

The first fire insurance company in Britain was started in an office in Threadneedle Street, London, by a man with the unlikely name of If-Jesus-Christ-had-not-died-for-thee-thou-hadst-been-damned Barebones, the son of the Parliamentarian Praise-God Barebones. Barebones Junior left his original profession of physician and, changing his name to Nicholas Barbon, moved into the building trade when the Great Fire of London in 1666 opened up new opportunities. Having made his fortune, Barbon ventured into the world of fire insurance, setting up the Phenix Fire Office in 1680. He also formed the world's first fire brigade in 1684, which protected the houses he insured. The untrained firemen were paid one shilling for the first hour and 6d for subsequent hours of firefighting, as well as all the beer they required. The business operated successfully until it was eventually wound up in 1712.

BRITAIN'S LAST STAND

The last battle fought on British soil was at Culloden Field, near Inverness on 16 April 1746, between Charles Stuart (Bonnie Prince Charlie, the Young Pretender) and the forces of King George II. The Jacobite rebels were defeated and the would-be king fled, disguised as a woman, having failed to restore the Stuarts to the throne.

The last battle fought on English soil was the Battle of Sedgemoor in Somerset, fought on 6 July 1685, when the forces of James II defeated those of the Duke of Monmouth, the illegitimate son of Charles II.

The last clan battle in Scotland was that between Clan Mackintosh and Clan MacDonald at Mulroy in 1688.

The bloodiest battle fought between the British on their own soil was the Battle of Towton in Yorkshire on 29 March 1461, when 36,000 Yorkists defeated 42,000 Lancastrians. The death toll is thought to have been around 28,000.

FAMOUS HORSES IN HISTORY

Horse	Rider
Black Agnes	Mary Queen of Scots
Black Bess	Dick Turpin
Copenhagen	Duke of Wellington
Lamri	King Arthur
Ronald	Lord Cardigan
Rosabelle	Mary Queen of Scots
Sorrel	William III
White Surrey	Richard III

LESSER-KNOWN BRITISH ECCENTRICS

Edward Hyde, third Earl of Clarendon (1661–1723)
It has long been rumoured that when Edward Hyde was
made governor of New Jersey by Queen Anne, he decided
that as the representative of a Queen, he should conduct
his job dressed as a woman, and turned up to his first function in a blue silk dress. Historians have since denounced
the tale and blamed the Earl's enemies for spreading
rumours of his transvestism (and those enemies did suc-
ceed in having him recalled to Britain). But to this day
there hangs in the New York Historical Society a portrait
of a very plain woman, who has never been identified;
the only marking is the word 'Clarendon' scratched on to
the frame.

GREAT BRITISH FIRSTS

In 1839, a blacksmith from Dumfries named Kirkpatrick
Macmillan invented the world's first bicycle. Known as a
velocipede, it was made of a wooden frame, the front of
which was carved into a horse's head, and it had iron-tyred
wheels. It was propelled by two rods connected to the back
wheel, which had to be pumped backwards and forwards.
Despite the weight of the bicycle – 57lb – Macmillan used
it to get him the 14 miles from Dumfries to Courthill. His
curious contraption led to the world's first cycling accident;
when he cycled the 40 miles or so to Glasgow, a crowd
turned out to see him and he accidentally knocked over a
small child, for which he was fined five shillings.

OLD PICTURE, NEW CAPTION

Edith discovers the downside of equal rights for women.

HISTORIC FIGURES COCKNEY-STYLE

Captain Cook *book*
Doctor Crippen *dripping*
Jack the Ripper *kipper*
Molly Malone *phone*
Oliver Twist *fist*
Richard the Third *bird*

THE IRISH NATIONAL ANTHEM

The Soldier's Song

We'll sing a song, a soldier's song,
With cheering rousing chorus,
As round our blazing fires we throng,
The starry heavens o'er us;
Impatient for the coming fight,
And as we wait the morning's light,
Here in the silence of the night,
We'll chant a soldier's song.

Chorus:

Soldiers are we whose lives are pledged to Ireland;
Some have come from a land beyond the wave.
Sworn to be free, no more our ancient sire land
Shall shelter the despot or the slave.
Tonight we man the gap of danger
In Erin's cause, come woe or weal
'Mid cannons' roar and rifles peal,
We'll chant a soldier's song.

In valley green, on towering crag,
Our fathers fought before us,
And conquered 'neath the same old flag
That's proudly floating o'er us.
We're children of a fighting race,
That never yet has known disgrace,
And as we march, the foe to face,
We'll chant a soldier's song. *[Chorus]*

Sons of the Gael! Men of the Pale!
The long watched day is breaking;
The serried ranks of Inisfail
Shall set the Tyrant quaking.
Our camp fires now are burning low;

24

See in the east a silv'ry glow,
Out yonder waits the Saxon foe,
So chant a soldier's song. *[Chorus]*

LOST OCCUPATIONS

Ale conner ....Inspector of beer and bread
Bowyer ....Maker or seller of archery bows
Broderer ....Person who embroiders
Bumbailiff ....Officer who collects debts
Cartwright .... Maker of carts
Colporteur ....Seller of books, especially bibles
Cooper ....Maker of barrels
Cordwainer ....Shoemaker, leather worker
Costermonger ....Fruit and vegetable salesman
Fletcher ....Maker of arrows
Goliard .... Wandering scholar
Gombeen man ....Irish moneylender
Horner ....Person who makes items out of horn
Scrivener ....Person who wrote out legal documents
Spelunker ....Explorer of caves
Wainwright ....Maker of carts

HOW MANY PECKS IN A BUSHEL?

The dry measure weights that time forgot
1 chaldron = 36 bushels
1 quarter = 8 bushels
1 bushel = 4 pecks
1 peck = 2 gallons
1 gallon = 4 quarts
1 quart = 2 pints
1 pint = 4 gills

ETHELRED THE UNFAIRLY NAMED

King Ethelred's nickname of 'Ethelred the Unready' has always suggested that he was a war-shy king, or a leader who was more likely to drag his feet than make bold and kingly decisions. In fact his nickname was originally 'Unred', meaning 'ill-advised'. This was an unkind pun on 'Ethelred', which means 'of noble counsel' or 'well advised'. Clearly the chroniclers of his time thought otherwise.

IN THE BLEAK MIDWINTER

On 20 January 1838, London was in the grip of a deep freeze. On this, the coldest day, a thermometer in Hyde Park measured -3°F (-19°C) at 6.30am, and never got much above 18°F (-14°C) all day. Amid the freeze, one Patrick Murphy, a weather prophet, made his appearance. A month or two earlier he had submitted the manuscript of his *Weather Almanac on Scientific Principles Showing the State of the Weather for Every Day of the Year of 1838*. He had predicted that January would be particularly severe and that the twentieth would most probably be the coldest day. When the accuracy of his prediction emerged, his publishers, Whittaker and Co, were inundated with requests for copies of the forthcoming book. Murphy made a tidy sum, even though by the end of the year he was found to have been right on only 167 days, and quite wrong on the rest. However, he based his predictions on his belief that the weather was dictated by the planets and stars. If he was wrong, he said, it was simply because the planets didn't do what they were supposed to do, for which he couldn't be held responsible. He continued to turn out the occasional weather almanac, none of which was any more accurate, until his death in 1847.

SHOOTING THE MESSENGER

In the thirteenth century, King Henry III struggled to exert power over the tribal princes of Wales, and came to various arrangements with them, in which he promised to leave them alone in return for the use of their men as troops. However, not everyone was receptive to his diplomacy. When Henry sent a summons to Walter de Clifford, Lord of Llandovery, de Clifford was so outraged by the King's presumption of authority over him that he forced the messenger to eat the summons – royal seal and all.

A DAY AT THE RACES

In 2005, a building company digging up a site in Colchester, Essex unearthed the remains of a Roman chariot-racing arena that dated back to around 50AD. Measuring 400 metres long by 60 metres wide, it was large enough to accommodate up to 8000 spectators. Historians believe that the riders would have had to complete about seven laps around the arena, which was two miles of racing. As well as the basic outline of the arena, archaeologists found pieces of horse trapping, horse jaws, a man's skeleton, a Roman coin and a stylus, which might have been used to write down bets. It is the largest Roman building in Britain, and apart from a similar complex found in Germany, it is the only large chariot-racing complex to have been found in northern Europe.

PAST PUZZLES

What will the following phrase help you to remember?
Can Queen Victoria Eat Cold Apple Pie?
Answer on page 145.

THE BUILDING OF HADRIAN'S WALL

In the year 122, the Emperor Hadrian decided to build an immense wall across the north of Britain, to divide the Roman-occupied territories in the south from unoccupied Caledonia to the north, where the Caledonian tribes remained unsubdued. Legionaries from the IInd Augusta, XXth Valeria Victrix and VIIth Victrix began to build the wall in 122, and took about 16 years to complete the task.

The wall ran for 80 Roman miles from Wallsend in the east to Bowness-on-Solway in the west. It was intended at first to be a series of signal stations, but ended up as a continuous wall with 16 forts (permanent quarters for garrisons), mile castles every mile for patrols and signal towers in between. It measured around eight feet deep and 15–20 feet high, and was protected by a ditch on its northern side and a flat-bottomed trench to the south. It was guarded by a garrison of around 20,000 soldiers. Parts of it were destroyed during various uprisings, but it was rebuilt by the Romans each time.

After the Romans left, the wall was often plundered for building materials, and much of it was destroyed during the construction of a major road from Newcastle to Carlisle in the 1750s. Since then, it has enjoyed better protection and is now looked after by various bodies such as the National Trust and English Heritage. It is much visited by ramblers, although few have matched the endeavours of one William Hutton from Birmingham, who in 1801 walked its entire length at the age of 79 and wrote a book about its history.

When Henry Tudor killed Richard III at the Battle of Bosworth in 1485, he claimed the throne on the grounds that he was a descendant of Edward III. This tenuous route to succession left Henry open to alternative claims upon the throne, the first of which came from a boy named Lambert Simnel.

Simnel landed in Ireland in 1487, claiming that he was the Earl of Warwick, Richard III's nephew, and had recently escaped from the Tower. He found willing supporters in Ireland, who crowned him king there, and plotted to place him on the English throne.

Simnel and his supporters launched a half-hearted invasion, but were easily defeated at the Battle of Stoke. Simnel was captured, and the real Earl of Warwick was temporarily removed from the Tower and paraded in public to dispel any confusion.

However, King Henry was so unthreatened by the incompetent claimant (not least because Simnel was barely 12 years old) that he put him to work in the royal kitchens, where it is alleged he invented a particularly delicious fruit cake that still bears his name. However, this is more likely to be coincidence than truth.

The second claimant had the equally unlikely name of Perkin Warbeck, who claimed to be Richard, Duke of York, the youngest of the famous princes imprisoned in the Tower. Warbeck took the precaution of securing the support of the Scottish king, James IV, and a group of English nobles before attempting to steal the throne. James IV began an invasion of England on Warbeck's behalf, but later expelled the pretender in fear of retaliation.

But it seemed that all the attention had gone to Warbeck's head, and he besieged Exeter in 1497. He was defeated, later captured and was executed in 1499.

HOW MONEY WAS MADE

In the year 1000 there were about 70 mints around England, producing soft silver alloy coins for public use. However, there was a catch; the coins were valid for only two or three years, and then they had to be taken back and exchanged for new ones. For every 10 that were handed in, you received only eight or nine in return, and the rest was kept by the government. The money-exchanger was therefore an early kind of tax-collector and sometimes, in more provincial areas, he also made the coins. He could have made more money by adding more alloy to the silver, but as the penalty for such fraud was to have his hand cut off and nailed to the wall of the mint, the temptation was easily resisted.

YORKSHIRE ROCK

Britain's famous Blackpool rock was first made not in Blackpool but in Yorkshire. In 1876, former miner Ben Bullock, who had set up in Dewsbury as a confectioner, came up with the idea of making a stick of sweet rock with words running through it. The first words he used were 'Whoa Emma', a popular music hall song of the time. He took some rock on holiday to Blackpool, and when it attracted the attention of local merchants, he made up a quantity of rock containing the word 'Blackpool'. Orders soon flooded in from home and overseas, and a great British tradition was born. Blackpool rock has continued to be part of our heritage, with only one small hiccup; a 1970s report on industrial sabotage told the sad tale of a consignment of rock that had to be thrown away when it was discovered that a four-letter obscenity ran through the centre of each stick, the work of a disgruntled employee.

OFF WITH THEIR HEADS

In early 2005, 56 skeletons were found in a Roman cemetery in York. The find itself was not unusual, but what puzzled archaeologists was that the skeletons' heads had been chopped off, despite the fact that the Romans had no tradition of decapitation. They concluded that the dead men may have been soldiers from what is now the Rhineland in Germany, who served under Emperor Septimus Severus in 200AD, and who had been buried according to tribal tradition, with their displaced skulls placed by their feet or legs. Dr Patrick Ottaway of the York Archaeological Trust said: 'Romans believed that the head was the seat of the soul, and they may have cut off their heads to stop them haunting the living.'

THE POWER OF SUPERSTITION

Had the Roman legions of 43AD given in to their irrational fears, the history of Britain might have been very different. At the time of the Roman invasion, the wisest minds insisted that the continent inhabited by the Romans was surrounded by empty oceans. Britain, however, was rising out of the water, which suggested that the island they sought to occupy was something mysterious, and perhaps not to be interfered with. So despite Julius Caesar's short foray into British territory in 55BC, the troops were unhappy. In 40AD, the Emperor Gaius assembled an invading army, but the army refused to sail. It was only three years later, after a near mutiny, that the soldiers of Aulus Plautius agreed to venture into the unknown and landed on the shores of first-century Britain.

CAR TROUBLE

The first man to drive a motor car on public roads in the UK was Henry Hewetson of Catford, who purchased a 2hp Benz from Mannheim and brought it home in November 1894. He drove around Catford for several weeks before being stopped by the police and informed that his automobile did not conform with the Locomotives on Highways Act 1865, which required him to have a man walking ahead of the car, waving a red flag. Infuriated by such petty rules, Hewetson employed two boys, one to travel in the car and one to go ahead by bicycle and keep an eye out for policeman. When an officer was spotted, the first boy signalled to the second boy, who hopped out of the car and strolled along in front of it, holding up a two-inch square of red linen attached to a small pencil.

DRINK TO ME ONLY

Drinks named after historic figures

Bloody Mary – vodka and tomato juice, created by Ferdinand Petiot of Harry's in New York and named after Queen Mary. It was first called Bucket of Blood, then The Red Snapper (when Worcestershire sauce, salt and pepper were added) before acquiring its royal name.

Grog – Vice Admiral Sir Edward Vernon wore a grogram coat on board ship and was known as Old Grog; when he ordered that the rum ration be watered down to reduce disorder aboard ship, the disgruntled sailors called it 'grog'.

Tom Collins – named after a nineteenth-century bartender from London, who created the mixture of gin, lemon, sugar and soda water.

Rob Roy – a mixture of whisky, sweet vermouth and bitters topped with a maraschino cherry, named after the legendary Scotsman.

OLD PICTURE, NEW CAPTION

Alexander Graham Bell learns that he is being held in a queue and will be answered shortly.

FAMOUS LAST WORDS

The parting words of some historic figures

What dost thou fear? Strike man, strike!
Sir Walter Raleigh, courtier, explorer and adventurer, to his executioner in 1618.

There are six guineas for you. And do not hack me as you did my Lord Russell.
Duke of Monmouth, the illegitimate son of Charles II, to his executioner in 1685.

It's all been very interesting.
Lady Mary Wortley Montagu, writer, feminist, socialite. Died 1762.

Too late for fruit, too soon for flowers.
Walter de la Mare, poet, on being asked if he would like fruit or flowers. Died 1956.

So now all is gone. Empire, body, soul.
King Henry VIII. Died 1547.

The devil do with it! It will end as it began; it came with a lass and it will go with a lass.
James V, King of Scotland. Died 1542.

Either that wallpaper goes, or I do.
Oscar Wilde, wit and dramatist. Died 1900.

Be of good cheer, Master Ridley, and play the man.
We shall this day light such a candle, by God's grace,
in England, as I trust shall never be put out.
Hugh Latimer, Bishop of Worcester, to Nicholas Ridley, Bishop of London, both burned at the stake by Mary I in 1555.

THE FIRST DIVORCE

The first civil divorce in England was granted in 1546, to separate a Lady Sadleir of Standon, Hertfordshire, from her first husband, Mr Barr. Formerly Mrs Margaret Barr, Lady Sadleir had remarried after Barr disappeared and was presumed dead, but he inconveniently reappeared after his wife had married Sir Ralph Sadleir. The Ecclesiastical Courts were alarmed; the second marriage could not be confirmed until the first was dissolved, and was clearly bigamous. Fortunately they gave Lady Sadleir the benefit of the doubt and accepted that she had remarried in good faith, but they had to go to the considerable lengths of putting a Private Bill through Parliament to allow her first marriage to be dissolved. It was to be the only civil divorce granted to a woman before 1801.

TWENTIETH-CENTURY CRISES

The Chanak Crisis, 1922

In September 1922, the British government became concerned that Mustapha Kemal (Ataturk) of Turkey would attack the Allied armies guarding the approach to Istanbul (then Constantinople). Kemal had recently defeated the Greeks at Smyrna, and the fear was that he would try to reclaim territory assigned to the Greeks in the 1920 Treaty of Sèvres, a treaty he had never accepted. The Prime Minister, Lloyd George, wanted to strengthen British forces serving at Chanak; but the crisis was avoided by an Anglo-Turkish agreement made in October that returned certain territories to Turkey, in return for its agreement not to pursue further territorial ambitions. The crisis, and the closeness of war with Turkey, was the downfall of Lloyd George, who found himself out of office two weeks after the agreement was signed.

A PLAGUE ON ALL YOUR HOUSES

The most famous plague in British history was the Black Death, possibly the greatest tragedy ever to hit western Europe. It began in Asia and was spread by rats who stowed away on the trading ships that linked Asia to Europe. This bubonic (glandular) plague soon ripped across the medieval world, reaching the south coast of Britain in 1348. Two of the first victims were Edward III's daughter, Joan, who died in Bordeaux in September of that year, and the Archbishop of Canterbury, who died a month earlier, proving that no one was safe. Nobility and peasantry alike were felled in their thousands. In the first year, the plague killed one-fifth of the entire population of Britain, and would eventually dispatch almost half the country. Worldwide, it claimed the lives of 75,000,000 people.

The illness struck quickly; black boils erupted under the skin in the groin and armpits, and sufferers were dead within a few days or hours. Men and women dropped dead in the street, and entire towns and cities were wiped out in days or weeks. The disease was so contagious that the healthy were forced to abandon the sick in order to survive, and families and communities were torn apart. Modern excavations of burial grounds show that bodies were simply piled into pits five or six deep and covered over, without ceremony. In a short-sighted tactic, the Scots saw an opportunity to launch an attack on the English, and gathered at Selkirk forest. But plague struck the camp, 5000 died, and the rest returned to Scotland, taking the disease with them. As the plague died down, the horror was not yet over. It returned in 1362, 1369 and 1375 to carry off the survivors of the first wave. Before 1348, the population of Britain was about 5,000,000; by the end of the century it was around 3,500,000 or less. Britain's population did not recover until the middle of the next century.

However, despite all the devastation, the plague did bring about changes that were of considerable benefit to the survivors. A shortage of labour meant that those who were left were in a strong position for negotiation; wages sometimes doubled, especially for farmhands who were producing food for what was left of the population. Landowners desperate for tenants had to improve their terms, and serfs who had previously worked for nothing now demanded wages and, eventually, their freedom. Many men who had been farming a tiny plot of land inherited the plots left by their dead relations, and found they were wealthy. The peasants also lost some of their respect for authority, not least because they had seen how readily the nobility and clergy had fled to safety, abandoning their tenants and flock. The plague would return with depressing regularity in the decades to come, but after this one terrible outbreak, things would never be quite the same again.

BRITISH RECORD-BREAKERS

Britain's tallest man: Patrick Cotter O'Brien (1760–1806) from County Cork: eight feet one inch. He was officially a giant, being over eight feet tall.

Tallest Scotsman: Angus Macaskill (1825–63) from Berneray in the Sound of Harris: seven feet nine inches.

Tallest Englishman: William Bradley (1787–1820) born in Market Weighton, East Yorkshire: seven feet nine inches.

Tallest Welshman: William Evans (1599–1634) of Gwent, porter to King James I: seven feet six inches.

WOMEN IN BRITISH POLITICS

1553 The first queen to rule alone is crowned: Mary I, 'Bloody Mary'. (Henry I declared his daughter Matilda his heir and she took control of the country for a few months in 1141, but was never crowned. Lady Jane Grey was declared queen in 1553, but was deposed within nine days and was never crowned.)

1903 The Women's Social and Political Union founded by Emmeline Pankhurst and daughters Christabel and Sylvia.

1909 Elizabeth Garrett Anderson is elected Mayor of Aldeburgh, Suffolk, and is the first woman to become mayor.

1918 Women are given the vote (if aged 30 and over) and for the first time women could be elected as MPs.

1918 Constance, Countess Markiewicz, is the first woman to be elected to Parliament. Elected MP for Sinn Fein, she was unable to take her seat, as she was in prison.

1919 The first woman takes her seat in the House of Commons: Nancy Astor, the Conservative MP for Plymouth South.

1928 The voting age is made the same for women and men for the first time.

1929 Margaret Bondfield becomes the first woman to be a Cabinet Minister; she is appointed Minister for Labour in the Labour minority government.

1955 Dame Evelyn Sharp becomes the first woman to be head of a department in the Civil Service.

1979 Margaret Thatcher, Conservative, becomes the UK's first female Prime Minister.

1992 Betty Boothroyd, appointed on 27 April, is the first woman to be made Speaker of the House of Commons.

THE WAGES OF SIN

Laura Bell, a former shop assistant from Belfast, could arguably claim the title of London's most expensive prostitute. In 1850 she charged the prime minister to the Maharaja of Nepal £250,000 to spend one night with her. He paid up. She later married the nephew of the Bishop of Norwich and became a preacher. She was preceded in her profession by the equally bold Kitty Fisher, whose nightly fee was 100 guineas, and who once threw the Duke of York out of bed for trying to pay her with a mere £50 note. She baked the note in a pie and ate it for breakfast. She finally embraced respectability by marrying an MP in 1765.

BRITAIN'S ROYAL ASTRONOMERS

John Flamsteed *1675–1719*
Edmund Halley *1720–1742*
James Bradley *1742–1762*
Nathaniel Bliss *1762–1764*
Nevil Maskelyne *1765–1811*
John Pond *1811–1835*
Sir George Airy *1835–1881*
Sir William Christie *1881–1910*
Sir Frank Dyson *1910–1933*
Sir Harold Jones *1933–1955*
Sir Richard Woolley *1956–1971*
Sir Martin Ryle *1972–1982*
Sir Francis Graham-Smith *1982–1990*
Sir Arnold Wolfendale *1991–1995*
Sir Martin Rees *1995–*

SCHOOL'S OUT

The age at which a child could leave school in the UK

1870	10 years
1899	12 years
1918	14 years
1944	15 years
1973	16 years

Other educational milestones

1870 Education provided for all children over five.
1880 School attendance made compulsory.
1891 State education provided free of charge.
1944 Education divided into primary and secondary levels.
1944 Eleven-plus exam introduced.
1965 Comprehensive schools first established.
1988 National Curriculum drawn up (revised in 1994).

STRANGE CUSTOMS

The Boys' Ploughing Match, Orkney

This centuries-old contest has its roots in Norse tradition – Orkney remained under Danish rule until well into the Middle Ages. On the third Saturday in August, on the tiny island of South Ronaldsay, boys and girls dress up as horses in traditional costume, which has often been passed down through the generations. After the horse costumes have been judged, the 'ploughmen' – boys under the age of 15 – line up on the beach at the Sands O'Right with their miniature ploughs, again often family heirlooms, and compete for the best furrow ploughed in the sand. The results are judged very solemnly with points given for straightest line, neatest ends and best starts.

THE SOMERSET TSUNAMI

In 1607, an enormous wave roared up the Bristol Channel and burst over the coast of Somerset, sweeping away villages, bridges, people and livestock. The wave flooded hundreds of square miles of land, drowned 2000 people and was seized upon by religious pamphleteers as an opportunity to warn against invoking the wrath of God. William Jones in his pamphlet *God's Warning to his People of England* claimed that the flood was the third of three dire warnings to England, preceded by the 1603 plague and the Gunpowder Plot. 'Many are the dombe warnings of destruction, which the Almighty God hath lately scourged this our kingdome with... all which, in bleeding hearts, may inforce us to put on the true garment of repentance,' he warned. The *Lamentable Newes* pamphlet agreed, laying the blame on idle gentry and clergy. 'The Cleargie doth nothing but looke for livings, and leave the labours of their function; and the Gentry esteeme more of their Hawkes, Houndes, and other their vainer pleasures then the godly discharging of their offices wherein the Lord hath set them,' it fumed. The catastrophe was a chance for the Puritans to vent their fury at attempts to relax anti-Catholic legislation and at the dismissal of Puritan clergy. But while their anger may have been justified, it was of little use to ordinary citizens, who had to wait a full 10 days before the waters receded and life could begin again.

HOME FROM HOME

The word 'Blighty', first used by British soldiers stationed in India to refer fondly to home, is a corruption of a Hindustani word *bilayati*, which means 'foreign country'.

PECULIAR PATRON SAINTS

St George of England was not English. He was probably Greek or Turkish, although his provenance has never been fully established.

St Patrick of Ireland was born at 'Bannavem Taberniae', part of Roman Britain, which we know from his own writings. This has been identified with many places, including Carlisle, Devon and Wales, but not anywhere in Ireland.

St Andrew of Scotland was one of Jesus's 12 disciples, which qualifies him for sainthood, but means he almost certainly wasn't Scottish.

St David of Wales was in fact the only native of the country for which he is a patron saint.

TRIBES OF ROMAN BRITAIN

In the late first century BC, tribes were emerging all over Britain, as the people settled and began to establish communities. In the first century AD, the tribes comprised the following:

Atrebates • Boresti • Brigantes • Caledonii
Careni • Carnonacae • Cantiaci • Carvetii
Catuvellauni • Coritani • Cornavii • Cornovii
Creones • Decantae • Deceangli • Demetae
Dobunni • Dumnonii • Durotriges • Epidii
Iceni • Lugi • Novantae • Ordovices • Parisi
Selgovae • Silures • Smertae • Taexali
Trinovantes • Vacomagii • Venicones • Votadini

GREAT BRITONS

Captain James Cook (1728–1779)

Captain Cook was one of the world's greatest explorers. Born in Yorkshire, he was apprenticed to a shopkeeper but left his post for the more exciting life of a sailor. After gaining experience on trading vessels, he joined the Navy and in 1759 was given the difficult task of charting the channel of the St Lawrence River in Canada, an experience that was to prove invaluable. In 1766, Cook was commissioned by the government to sail to the Pacific and observe the transit of Venus, and he set off in 1768 on the first of his three great voyages. He sailed around Cape Horn to discover New Zealand and on to the east coast of Australia, which he claimed for King George III. He returned home via New Guinea and the Cape, although the journey was blighted by dysentery and malaria among his crew. In 1772, Cook set sail again, this time for New Zealand via the Antarctic, sailing back to and around the South Pole before returning home in 1775, crossing a greater expanse of sea than any man had before. His third voyage, in 1776, took him past New Zealand and on around the world to America. After further expeditions to the Arctic Circle, Cook returned to Hawaii, where the natives were at first welcoming. But then trouble broke out and in a scuffle on the beach, Cook was stabbed in the back by one of the natives and fell dead. His body was dismembered by the natives, but his crew demanded that they return his remains, and they buried what was left of him at sea. Despite his historic and courageous achievements, Cook described himself simply as 'a plain man, zealously exerting himself in the service of his country'.

THE LAST EXECUTION

The last people to be executed in the UK were Peter Anthony Allen and John Robson Walby on 13 August 1964. In 1965 the death penalty was suspended for five years, and then abolished in 1969, with an exception for treason and piracy with violence. A powerful factor in its abolition was the hanging of Derek Bentley, a 19-year-old man with a much younger mental age, whose 16-year-old friend shot and killed a policeman. It was claimed that Bentley had shouted 'Let him have it!' although it was also argued that he meant for his friend to give up his gun. A few years earlier a man named Timothy Evans had been hanged for murdering his wife and child, although it was later thought that convicted murderer John Christie might have been the culprit, as they had lived at the same house. The death penalty for all crimes was finally abolished in the UK in 1999.

The youngest person ever to be executed in Britain was an eight-year-old boy, hanged for arson in the 1600s. The last child to be executed in Britain was hanged in 1887, although the execution of children was not officially outlawed until 1933.

THE IMPERIAL SIZE OF A FIELD

1 square mile = 640 acres
1 acre = 10 sq chains = 4 roods
1 rood = 40 sq poles
1 sq pole = 30¼ sq yards
1 sq yard = 9 sq feet
1 sq foot = 144 sq inches

OLD PICTURE, NEW CAPTION

Lady Fortescue was delighted to find that her new lorgnettes added a good 50 yards to her chaperoning range.

OLD PICTURE, NEW CAPTION

While Alfred was very proud of his newfangled plane, his wife was less than happy with the inflight facilities.

PAST PUZZLE

What was the Alexandra limp?
Answer on page 145.

THE REAL CAMELOT

One of the main claimants to the 'true' location of King Arthur's fabled Camelot is South Cadbury Hill in Somerset, a hill fort dating back to at least the pre-Roman Iron Age and occupied variously until the Saxon period. Its advocates point to its proximity to Glastonbury, which many believe was the Isle of Avalon, as well as to the recent discovery on the site of some post holes for what was once a large timber hall. This evidence further suggests that it was occupied and refortified by a post-Roman nobleman of great standing, who could possibly have been Arthur. Local folklore includes several Arthurian legends, including the most famous – that Arthur and his knights are just sleeping below the hill, ready to awake and defend England once more when the country is in peril. But one of the main arguments for Cadbury being Camelot is that the place names fit perfectly – Queen's Camel, West Camel, the River Cam and so on. However, the flaw in the argument is that while the Somerset villages are indeed ancient, the name Camelot was invented by the French poet Chrétien de Troyes in the twelfth century.

KEEN AS MUSTARD

The first mustard to be made in paste form rather than seed form was sold in London in 1720 by a Mrs Clements. The jars were covered with parchment cut from legal documents, giving rise to the joke that deeds and contracts are 'only fit to cover mustard pots'.

HOW ENGLISH IS ENGLISH?

The many occupiers of the British Isles, as well as forays into other lands by British explorers, have ensured that the Queen's English has a very mixed bag of origins indeed. Here is a handful of the most well known 'borrowings' from places around the world:

The Americas:
anorak, barbecue, buccaneer, cannibal, chilli, chocolate, hammock, hurricane, parka, pecan, poncho, potato, tobacco, toboggan, tomato

Africa:
banjo, commando, jazz, juke(box), mumbo-jumbo, raffia, trek, voodoo, zombie

Asia (western):
admiral, alchemy, alcohol, algebra, almanac, alphabet, arsenal, assassin, behemoth, caravan, checkmate, cherub, coffee, divan, hallelujah, hazard, horde, kiosk, lemon, leviathan, magazine, magic, mammoth, mogul, paradise, pyjamas, sequin, sofa, spinach, syrup, tariff, tiara, tulip, turkey, zenith, zero

Southern and south-eastern Asia:
bungalow, caddy, chintz, chutney, compound, crimson, dinghy, dungaree, gingham, guru, gymkhana, juggernaut, jungle, junk, lacquer, loot, mandarin, mantra, pariah, pundit, sapphire, shampoo, sugar, swastika

Central and eastern Asia:
china, chin-chin, gung-ho, judo, kamikaze, ketchup, kowtow, tea, tycoon

Europe (Germanic):
anger, balderdash, bluff, blunder, boss, bully, bumpkin, coleslaw, cookie, dapper, doze, egg, fellow, flimsy, frolic, golf, grime, hamster, inkling, loiter, muck, nasty, nudge, oaf, poppycock, rant, scowl, smack, smuggle, spook, ugly, window, yacht

Europe (Greek):
agnostic, analyst, antithesis, automaton, biology, blasphemy, charisma,

cinema, crisis, criterion, critic, diagnosis, dinosaur, dogma, drama, electron, enigmatic, genesis, hoi polloi, patriarch, phenomenon, photograph, stigma, synthesis

Europe (Latin):

apex, area, bacteria, camera, circus, complex, equilibrium, formula, fungus, genius, inertia, interim, medium, momentum, opera, pauper, pendulum, propaganda, referendum, series, simile, status, vertigo, victor

Europe (Romance languages):

anchovy, barricade, battalion, beauty, brochure, camouflage, castle, charlatan, chivalry, conquest, defeat, design, dessert, dinner, embargo, garage, garden, honest, loyal, morale, mutton, nutmeg, palaver, paste, poison, prestige, quest, royal, souvenir, tempest, ticket

ROYAL FLUSH

In 1953, in preparation for the coronation of Queen Elizabeth II, a number of extra toilets were installed at Westminster Abbey to save any undignified queuing on the part of the distinguished guests. But at some point before the big day, someone had a horrible thought. If all the toilets were occupied and flushed at once at a particularly solemn point in the ceremony, would the noise be captured by the BBC's sound equipment as they televised the event? The prospect was too awful to contemplate. The organisers decided that this scenario had to be tested, and a group of Guards from the nearby Wellington Barracks was summoned to the Abbey and assigned a toilet each. A number of BBC technicians were equipped with decibel meters and arranged along the line, and the order was given for all the toilets to be flushed at once. Fortunately, it was discovered that no sound could be heard inside the Abbey walls, and the nation was spared an embarrassing moment that would have become an indelible part of Britain's history.

THEY SAY IT'LL BE OVER BY CHRISTMAS

The longest wars in which Britain fought

The Hundred Years War lasted 116 years, from 1337–1453
The Wars of the Roses lasted 30 years, from 1455–1485
The Thirty Years War lasted 30 years, from 1618–1648
The Napoleonic Wars lasted 23 years, from 1792–1815

PRIDE BEFORE A FALL

The world's first traffic island was thought up by a Colonel Pierpoint, who had it constructed outside his London club on St James's Street in 1864. He would often turn to admire it as he crossed, which caused him on one occasion to be knocked down by a car while heading for his club.

THE COST OF WAR

Estimated figures for World Wars One and Two*

Number of British combatants killed in
World War One 743,000
Number of British combatants killed in
World War Two...468,000
Total combatant death toll of World War One,
all countries 15,000,000
Total combatant death toll of World War Two,
all countries 65,000,000

Based on the best estimates. The true cost may never be known.

Robert Nixon

To most people, Robert Nixon seemed like a simpleton. Gangly and almost mute, with an enlarged head and bulging eyes, he was an odd addition to the Cholmondeley household of 1485, capable only of ploughing their fields. But Robert had a special talent – he could predict the future. His first predictions were simple ones, such as the death of a neighbour's ox. But he soon began to work on a grander scale and predicted the Great Plague, the 1666 fire of London, the beheading of Charles I, the reign of William of Orange and the French Revolution. His only fear seemed to be that his employers would starve him to death – he had a vast appetite and had to be watched in case he ate himself sick.

When Robert predicted the defeat of Richard III at the Battle of Bosworth two days before it happened, his genius reached the ears of the new king, Henry VII. The king sent for Robert and gave him a scribe to write down his predictions. Sadly, before the king could actually meet his new prophet, Robert's greatest fear was realised; a furious cook, tired of finding the boy stealing food, locked him in a cupboard and forgot about him. His body was found two weeks later.

LONG IN THE TOOTH

In 1816, one of Sir Isaac Newton's teeth was sold for £730 to an anonymous nobleman in London. He had the tooth set in a ring, which he then wore for the rest of his life.

MIND THE STAIRS

The first escalator in the UK was installed in Harrods department store in London, at the instigation of the manager, Richard Burbage, who disliked elevators. To soothe the nerves of first-time users, an attendant was positioned at the top to dispense brandy and sal volatile. Anyone who didn't shop at Harrods was able to try the escalator installed at Crystal Palace in south-east London, for a penny a ride.

The first escalators to be installed on the Underground were at Earls Court Station in 1911. Notices were posted warning passengers not to sit on the stairs, and to step off with the left leg first. To reassure the nervous, a man with a wooden leg known as 'Bumper' Harris was employed to ride up and down all day to demonstrate the ease and safety of the new invention. But the authorities needn't have worried; the *Illustrated London News* reported that passengers were often seen getting off a train and riding up the stairs and down again before getting back on the next train.

SUFFERING SUFFRAGETTES

Marion Wallace Dunlop, a suffragette, was the first person to go on hunger strike in Britain, after she was imprisoned in 1909 for painting a clause from the Bill of Rights on the walls of the House of Commons. She was released after fasting for 91 hours. The next suffragettes who tried the same thing were force-fed until a public outcry ended the barbaric practice. However, the government then passed the Prisoners' Temporary Discharge for Ill-health Act in 1913, which was known as the Cat and Mouse Act. Suffragettes were released when the fasting made them ill, but were re-arrested when they recovered, which was hardly an improvement. Women finally won the right to vote in 1918.

FAMOUS LAST WORDS

The parting words of some historic figures:

I desire to leave to the men that come after me a remembrance of me in good works.
Alfred the Great, King of Wessex. Died in 899.

I will die King of England. I will not budge a foot. Treason! Treason!
King Richard III, killed at the Battle of Bosworth by Henry Tudor's troops. Died in 1485.

In vain you menace me. If all the swords in England were brandishing over my head, your terrors did not move me.
Thomas á Becket, Archbishop of Canterbury, killed in Canterbury Cathedral for challenging the authority of King Henry II. Died in 1170.

Shame, shame on a conquered king!
King Henry II, referring to the fact that his sons were conspiring against him with the King of France. Died in 1189.

The executioner is, I believe, very expert. And my neck is very slender. Oh God have pity on my soul!
Anne Boleyn, second wife of King Henry VIII. Died in 1536.

HANG ON, HELP IS ON ITS WAY

In 1705, a burglar named John Smith was hanged at Tyburn Tree. He had been suspended for a full 15 minutes when a reprieve arrived, and he was hurriedly cut down and revived. Astonishingly he survived, as the drop had not broken his neck. He was known afterwards as Half-Hanged Smith.

A WELSH HISTORY TEST

In March 2005, *The Times* reported that the manager of the Welsh rugby team, Alan Phillips, had compiled a black book called the *Protocol Book,* which he hoped would instil a sense of Welsh pride into his players. The players were expected to commit the contents to memory and were tested at random. As well as key points in Welsh history, it included famous speeches, battles, folklore and, of course, rugby history. The following facts were included:

- Llantwit Major is the oldest university town in Britain.
- Las Vegas was mostly founded by Welsh Mormons.
- The first shots in the English Civil War were fired at Pembroke Castle.
- Colonel Mainwaring, a Welshman, invented lawn tennis.
- The world's highest mountain is named after a Welshman – Sir George Everest.
- The last Briton to die in World War One was Able Seaman Richard Morgan, from Gwent.
- Jack Daniels Bourbon, Evans Williams Bourbon and Mathews Southern Comfort were all Welsh brewers who left Wales during the temperance period.
- Welshmen may have settled in America before Columbus.
- Tying a yellow ribbon around a tree was an eighteenth-century Welsh tradition, practised by settlers to help other Welshmen who had travelled to a new land to find their countrymen.

INFLATED VALUES

On 22 April 1659, the first cheque to be drawn on a British bank was made out to the bearer by one Nicholas Vanacker, for the sum of £10. The original cheque was sold at Sotheby's for £1300 in 1976.

TABLE MANNERS

Unacceptable behaviour at the medieval dinner table:

- Eating before everyone has been served and the lord of the manor has taken his first mouthful.

- Dipping one's bread in the soup.

- Leaving a soup spoon in the dish (it should be wiped and placed back on the table).

- Taking half-eaten food out of the mouth and putting it back on the plate.

- Dipping meat into the salt dish.

- Tipping the leftover fat from the dish on to the tablecloth.

- Licking the plate clean.

- Using a knife to pare the nails or pick the teeth.

- Wiping the knife on the tablecloth.

- Spitting on the table rather than on the ground.

- Wiping hands on the tablecloth (they should be wiped on the clothes instead).

- Using a napkin to blow one's nose.

- At the end of the meal, guests were expected to listen to grace being said, wash their hands and bow to the lord of the manor, saying 'Much good do it ye' before leaving the table.

WHO WAS THE REAL ST GEORGE?

It has always been a puzzle that St George, patron saint of England, was not an Englishman. So who was he? It was long thought that he was a Greek Prince, but this has been disputed by modern historians. It is known that he was a soldier and that he was tortured and beheaded for his Christian beliefs, supposedly at Lydda in Palestine about 304AD. But that is almost all that is known about him. It would seem that a legend has been created from a few vital details – Christian, soldier, hero – and has been embellished until it fits our requirements of a patriotic hero.

George was officially designated the patron saint of England by Pope Benedict IV (900–903), and from that point Britain accepted him as one of their own. English churches were dedicated to him, notably Doncaster in 1061. The Crusades of the thirteenth century then added to George's popularity, as his image was used as a symbol of English Christianity and of heroism. William of Malmesbury, the great medieval chronicler, said that St George and St Demetrius, 'the martyr knights', were 'seen' assisting the Franks at the battle of Antioch in 1098. It is also generally accepted that the 'arms of St George' (a red cross on a white shield) were introduced about the time of Richard the Lionheart (Richard I). In 1284, the armorial seal of Lyme Regis contained a ship flying a plain flag, bearing a cross, and the large red St George's cross on a white ground is still the 'White Ensign' of the Royal Navy. It is also, of course, one of the elements of the Union Flag. In the fourteenth century, St George's arms were officially adopted by English soldiers and sailors. Finally, King Edward III made St George the principal patron of the Order of the Garter, which the King founded around 1348, thus establishing the iconic status of this mysterious Christian knight.

FOR THE WIPING OF ONE'S NOSE

Next time you blow your nose, you can thank Richard II, as it was he who is credited with bringing the handkerchief to England. His wardrobe accounts were in Latin, but when transcribed, they described this peculiar new affectation as: 'Made of small pieces for the Lord King to carry in his hand for wiping and cleaning his nose.' It took a while to catch on and did not find favour for another hundred years or so. Richard, with an eye to the niceties of life, also introduced the novelties of individual, rather than communal, toilets and small fireplaces in the rooms of his courtiers.

THE EARLIEST ATKINS

The first formal slimming diet known in the UK was devised in 1862 by a Dr Harvey, for an overweight undertaker named William Banting. The diet consisted of the following:

Breakfast	4oz lean meat, fish or bacon; 1 oz toast
Dinner	A little more meat; vegetables (not potatoes), fruit, 1 oz toast
Tea	Tea without milk, a rusk, fruit
Supper	4oz meat or fish

This low-carbohydrate diet was not dissimilar to the famous Atkins diet, and it worked very nicely for Banting; within a year he had reduced his weight from 203lb to 153lb and extolled the virtues of the diet to anyone who would listen. His success gave rise to a new verb 'to bant', meaning to lose weight. But, unlike the practice of dieting, the word soon fell out of fashion.

STRANGE CUSTOMS

Red Hose Race

In Carwath in Strathclyde every August, a race is run in which all the participants have to wear red woollen stockings. The tradition dates back to 1508, when King James IV granted the lands and barony of Carnwath to Lord Somerville. The terms of the grant stated that the owner of Carnwath must, as part of his rent, pay 'one pair of hose containing half an ell of English cloth at the feast of Saint John the Baptist called Midsummer, to the man running most quickly from the east end of the town of Carnwath to the cross called Cawlo Cross'. While this may seem like a mischievous forfeit, it may have had something to do with training messengers to give warnings of raids on their border, although that doesn't explain why they didn't do so on horseback. The tradition has been continued ever since, as the estate would in theory be forfeited if this 'rent' were not paid. During the two world wars and the Foot and Mouth outbreaks of 1926 and 1952, permission had to be secured in writing from the Crown Authorities for the race to be suspended. Some details of the race have changed over the years; the distance has been reduced from three miles to one and it is held in August rather than midsummer. And instead of the waist-high blue cloth hose that was specified in the original grant, the runners now wear red woollen tights, knitted by the villagers.

LAST REQUEST

When George Bernard Shaw died in 1950, he requested in his will that his trustees commission a new 40-letter alphabet to rid the language of its difficult spellings. The alphabet was duly designed, but it failed to catch on. His only work to be published using the new alphabet was a version of *Androcles and the Lion*, published by Penguin in 1962.

HATS OFF

The bowler hat was invented in 1849 by Thomas and William Bowler, felt hatmakers of Southwark Bridge Road, to fulfil an order placed by Lock & Co of St James's. William Coke of Holkham, Norfolk, a customer of Lock & Co, was in need of a hat that would protect his head from overhanging branches while he was out shooting and Lock & Co commissioned the Bowlers to solve the problem. When Coke travelled to London on 17 December 1849 to collect his hat, he placed it on the ground and stamped on it firmly, twice, to test its resilience. The hat was undamaged, and Coke paid his 12 shillings. Although the rest of the world refers to the hat as a bowler, Lock & Co still refer to it as a Coke.

THE TROUBLE WITH MERCENARIES

After the Romans departed in 409, Britain's various kings were once again left to protect their own territories. According to legend, one such king, Vortigern, made the mistake of hiring mercenaries to do his fighting for him, not imagining that they might get a taste for their spoils. The most famous of these were the brothers Hengist and Horsa. Vortigern was impressed by their work and granted them the Isle of Thanet in place of the 'wages' he had promised. Furious, they rampaged through Britain, collecting their own rewards. Having lost his grip, Vortigern was then overthrown by his own son and sent into exile. Which just goes to show that it pays to fight your own battles.

HOW TO MEASURE YOUR PINT OF ALE

How we measured liquid before the litre

1 tun = 2 butts
1 butt = 2 hogsheads
1 hogshead = 1½ barrels
1 barrel = 2 kilderkins
1 kilderkin = 2 firkins
1 firkin = 9 gallons
1 gallon = 4 quarts
1 quart = 2 pints
1 pint = 4 gills
1 gill = 5 fluid ounces
1 fluid ounce = 8 fluid drachms
1 fluid drachms = 60 minims

WHAT'S IN A NAME?

When the Angles, Jutes and Saxons swept into Britain after 450, anyone who opposed them was shunted off into Cornwall, Wales, Scotland and Ireland, a crescent of rebellion popularly known as the Celtic Fringe. The Anglo-Saxons took over the rest of the country, and referred to the rebels as 'wealisc', which means 'foreign' – and which later became, simply, 'Welsh'. The Saxons began to refer to themselves as Angles, from which came 'Angleland', which became 'Engla-lond' and, finally, 'England'. But the Scots referred to the Saxon invaders as 'Sassenach', which remains, centuries later, a Scottish term of abuse.

FIVE DEGREES OF NOBILITY

Britain's ranks of nobility in order of importance

Duke
Introduced to England by Edward III.
First: Edward, Prince of Wales, made Duke of Cornwall in 1337.
Title: His Grace

Marquess
Introduced to England by Richard II.
First: Robert de Vere, made Marquess of Dublin in 1385.
Title: Most Honourable

Earl
An ealdorman administered a shire or province for the king; the title became hereditary under the Normans.
First: Roger Mortimer (the first for whom the title did not derive from a county or city), made Earl of March in 1328.
Title: Right Honourable

Viscount
Once the name for a deputy or lieutenant, it was made a degree of honour by Henry VI, and viscounts were created by patent.
First: John, Lord Beaumont (first to be created by patent) made Viscount Beaumont in 1440.
Title: Right Honourable

Baron
Originally a Norman title for landowners. In the thirteenth century barons were called to parliament to represent their area, and the title became part of the peerage.
First: John de Beauchamp, (first to be created by patent, by Richard II) made Baron of Kidderminster in 1387.
Title: Right Honourable

THE ORIGINS OF INCOME TAX

While we accept income tax as a part of British life, it was not introduced until as late as 1799, when Pitt levied it as a way of paying for the French Revolutionary War. The rate then was two shillings in the pound. It was abolished in 1802, but quickly reinstated in 1803 by Addington, although at the lower rate of one shilling in the pound. There it remained until 1816. Then in 1842, Peel introduced a rate of seven pence in the pound for three years. Gladstone was planning to abolish it by 1860, but had his plans upset by the Crimean War, when the rate rose to one shilling and fourpence. It continued to be thought of as a temporary measure throughout Victoria's reign, and the rate remained low. Both Gladstone and Disraeli raised hopes that it might be abolished in the 1874 election – at which time the rate was only fourpence – but instead it became a relied-upon source of revenue, and has remained so ever since, with PAYE being introduced in 1944. In World War One the rate rose to six shillings and later to ten shillings. The highest rate ever imposed on an ordinary public was 98p in the £1 in the 1970s.

GREAT BRITISH FIRSTS

In 1936, 19-year-old Daphne Kearley became the UK's first air hostess. She was paid £3 a week to look after passengers on the flight from Croydon to Le Bourget. She had to be able to cook, mix cocktails, speak French, take dictation and type, as her wealthy business-class passengers would dictate letters to her en route. She also enjoyed the perk of eating first-class meals, which often included salmon and caviar. She later reported that during her first 10 months in the job, she received 299 proposals of marriage.

SING A SONG OF HISTORY

Nursery rhymes and children's songs often commemorate famous historic people and events. Here are three popular interpretations:

Old King Cole – There was an Old King Coel in Britain in the late fourth and early fifth century, who ruled the northern Britons. However, he was not the only Coel around at this time, which has given rise to some confusion about his being the Lord of Colchester, which was another Coel altogether. As for the 'fiddlers three', there is no record that Coel was musical, nor that he was even a merry old soul.

The Grand Old Duke of York – this is most likely to have been Richard, Duke of York, who was killed in the Wars of the Roses. At the Battle of Wakefield in 1460, Richard marched his troops up to Sandal Castle, which was at the top of a hill, and at some point marched down again, abandoning his safe haven to make a direct attack. It failed, and he was killed.

Three Blind Mice – Queen Mary, known as Bloody Mary, owned vast estates with her husband, Philip of Spain, hence the reference to a farmer's wife. The three blind mice were three Protestant noblemen convicted of conspiring against the Queen, who was a staunch Catholic. She in fact had them burned at the stake rather than dismembered.

WHAT'S THAT IN OLD MONEY?

1 guinea = 21 shillings
1 pound = 20 shillings
1 crown = 5 shillings
1 shilling = 12 pence
1 penny = 4 farthings

IN THE LINE OF DUTY

Constable William Grantham has the unfortunate distinction of being the first British policeman to be murdered while on duty. Patrolling in Somers Town in north London on 29 June 1830, the constable came across two drunken men fighting over a woman, who was watching the affray. Attempting to separate the combatants, he was knocked to the ground and kicked to death by all three.

A1 DRIVER

When registration plates were introduced in Britain in 1903, the much-coveted A1 number plate was secured by the 2nd Earl Russell for his 12hp Napier. The plate was bequeathed to a Trevor Laker of Leicester in 1950 and sold in August 1959 for £2500, which was given to charity.

HOW FAR IS THAT IN NAILS?

Imperial measures of distance:
1 mile = 1760 yards
1 furlong = 220 yards
1 cable = 600 feet
1 chain = 22 yards = 100 links
1 rod, pole or perch = 5½ yards
1 fathom = 6 feet
1 yard = 3 feet = 36 inches
1 foot = 12 inches
1 span = 9 inches
1 hand = 4 inches
1 nail = 2¼ inches (for cloth)
1 inch = $\frac{1}{36}$ of a yard

FAMOUS HISTORIC DOGS

Dog	Owner
Boatswain	Lord Byron
Bounce	Alexander Pope
Boy	Prince Rupert
Cabal	King Arthur
Dash	Charles Lamb
Diamond	Isaac Newton
Flush	Elizabeth Barratt Browning
Geist, Kaiser	Matthew Arnold
Hamlet, Maida	Sir Walter Scott
Mathe	Richard II
Rufus	Winston Churchill

SEXUAL PENALTIES

During his reign, King Canute attempted to change the rather casual Anglo-Saxon attitude to sex and marriage by introducing a law that if a woman committed adultery, she lost all her property to her husband and had her nose and ears cut off. Fortunately, his draconian law died with him. However, during the Dark Ages there was an interesting selection of fines available for cases of sexual misconduct or assault:

- For lying with a virgin who was merely a slave: 12 shillings
- For lying with a virgin who worked in the royal flour mill: 25 shillings (for reasons of hygiene, perhaps)
- For lying with a virgin who was a servant in the royal household: 50 shillings
- For fondling the breast of a woman without consent: 5 shillings
- For throwing a woman to the floor: 10 shillings
- For rape: 60 shillings (paid to the woman herself)

John Dee

Born in Wales in 1527, John Dee was the son of a court official. Educated at the new Cambridge University, he proved to be so clever that he was considered to be one of England's most learned men. So learned, in fact, that many thought him to be a wizard.

At the time, the country was in the hands of Queen Mary, who was busy expunging the nation of Protestants. Many would have preferred her half-sister, Elizabeth, to be on the throne, and Elizabeth lived in constant fear of her life. Fearing the worst, Robert Dudley, a supporter and suitor of Elizabeth, went to Dee to ask for his advice. Dee drew up the young woman's horoscope, and predicted that she would not, in fact, be beheaded by Mary as she feared, but would become queen. When Mary heard of the prophesy, she had Dee thrown into the Tower, along with Elizabeth and Dudley. Fortunately they escaped execution and when Mary died in 1558, leaving the throne free for Elizabeth, Dee's fortunes were restored and he was made Astrologer Royal. He chose a propitious date for Elizabeth's coronation and continued to advise the Queen, throughout her reign. In 1583, he predicted 'the appearing of the very great sea and many ships thereon', at which the queen ordered more ships to be built. When the Spanish Armada appeared off England's shores five years later, England was ready for them. Sadly, Dee also predicted the one thing that the Queen would not change; that she would neither marry nor produce an heir.

TWENTIETH-CENTURY CRISES

The Abdication Crisis (1936)

On 10 December 1936, King Edward VIII did the unthinkable and gave up his throne to marry the woman he loved, American divorcee Wallis Simpson. In a broadcast to his subjects, he offered his continued service to his country: 'If at any time in the future I can be found of service to His Majesty in a private station I shall not fail.' However, the ex-King and his wife were to be virtually exiled. The new King, George VI, refused to take his brother's calls. A financial settlement was offered to Edward on the condition that he never return to live in the UK. No member of the royal family attended the wedding and the couple – by now the Duke and Duchess of Windsor – were told that their descendants could not inherit the title HRH. When Edward made an ill-judged visit to meet Hitler in 1937, it soured relations even further, and a rumour began that the King might be restored to the throne should Germany ever win a war with Britain. Edward's intentions were probably quite the opposite, but he was in great danger of being used by the Nazis as a pawn. After some bad-tempered negotiation with his family, the Duke finally accepted the governorship of the Bahamas and took up residence there in 1940, out of reach of the Germans. Edward retired from the post in 1945 and moved to France, where he and his wife lived out their days. Despite the long years of frosty relations, Prince Charles and the Queen both visited the Duke before he died in 1972, and his body was flown back to England and buried in Windsor. The Duchess died in 1986 and was buried beside her husband.

The Hervey family can lay claim to some of the country's most creative rogues and eccentrics:

John, Lord Hervey of Ickworth had manners so effeminate that he was referred to by Alexander Pope as Lord Fanny. Lord Hervey had a wife, mistresses and male lovers, and once turned his wife and children out of the family home so that he could give it to his lover, Stephen Fox.

Augustus Hervey, son of the second Earl of Bristol, was married at the age of 16, but kept it secret for 20 years so that his wife would not lose her job as maid of honour to the Princess of Wales. Hervey joined the navy and used his position to seduce a vast number of women, including some of the inhabitants of a convent in Odivellas. He once had to lie still under his lover's bedclothes while her husband bid her goodnight. He acknowledged only one child, although the boy was killed while serving in the Navy.

Frederick Hervey, the fourth Earl of Bristol and the Earl-Bishop of Derry once dropped a tureen full of pasta from a tower in Siena on to a Corpus Christi procession. He was also once imprisoned in a tower in Milan. When he died in Italy, the crew of the ship that was to transport his corpse refused to carry it, so the body was disguised in a packing case and sent home as an antique statue.

Victor Hervey, the sixth Marquess of Bristol, once drove his car into a taxi rank to satisfy his curiosity as to whether a taxi would buckle like a concertina. He discovered that they did. As well as writing gossip columns, in which he referred to himself as 'Mayfair Playboy No. 1', he worked (unsuccessfully) as a gun-runner in the Spanish Civil War, sold arms to China and lived as a tax exile in Monaco.

WHO ARE YOU CALLING A DUNCE?

John Duns Scotus (c.1266–1308) was a Scottish Franciscan who lectured in Oxford and Paris and was considered a highly sophisticated thinker for his time. He is considered to be the first person to drive a wedge between philosophy and theology, paving the way for the growth of scepticism in the fourteenth century. It seems strange, therefore, that he gave rise to the word 'dunce'. Scotists – a name given to those following his line of thinking – were also referred to as 'Dunsmen' or 'dunses', which, despite today's connotations, at first referred to someone who made 'impossibly ingenious distinctions', and could be taken as a compliment. However, it became a term of contempt after Duns's death, as his followers became best known for being deeply conservative and for blindly resisting change or new ideas.

TREASURES OF THE DEEP

In March 2005, a team of amateur archaeologists uncovered the find of a lifetime – the remains of a shipwreck believed to date back to 1300BC. Discovered in a mere 60 feet of water off the coast of Devon, the find offered an unprecedented insight into the behaviour of Britain's Bronze Age inhabitants. The South West Maritime Archaeological Group who found the remains, retrieved a cauldron hanger, bronze swords and axes and a solid gold torc, which suggest that the vessel was a warship rather than a trading ship. Sadly there was no trace of the wooden ship itself, which had long since disintegrated, but the artefacts were in exceptionally good condition. Only two other vessels of a similar age have been found, and it is possible that the Devon ship is one of the oldest shipwrecks to be found off the British coast.

THREE THINGS WALTER RALEIGH
DIDN'T DO

...lay down his cloak for Queen Elizabeth. The myth probably originated with imaginative historian Thomas Fuller, and was embroidered by Sir Walter Scott.

...introduce the potato to England. According to John Gerard's 1597 book *Herball*, the potato was first grown in Italy in 1585, and was introduced to England from there by Sir Francis Drake in 1586.

...introduce tobacco from America. Walter Raleigh never actually landed on mainland America, and Europe's first tobacco was brought from Brazil to France by Andre Thevet in 1556. The first tobacco to reach England came in on the ship of Sir John Hawkins c.1564. Sir Walter Raleigh was first introduced to tobacco by Sir Francis Drake some 20 years later.

NO PLACE LIKE HOME

The 10 most common placenames in Britain:

Name	No of occurrences
Newton	150
Blackhill	136
Castlehill	128
Mountpleasant	126
Woodside	112
Newtown	110
Burnside	107
Greenhill	105
Woodend	101
Beacon Hill	95

OLD PICTURE, NEW CAPTION

*At first, many were fooled by the French
army's inflatable decoys.*

WHO WAS THE REAL SHERIFF
OF NOTTINGHAM?

History has long enjoyed representing the Sheriff of Nottingham as an out-and-out villain. In fact, Nottingham didn't actually have a sheriff until 1449, although there had been a Sheriff of Nottinghamshire since the Conquest. However, that doesn't mean the story is mere fiction. In the supposed time of Robin Hood, while King Richard was away on the Crusades (1190–94), Nottingham was in a state of flux. Justiciar Longchamp (who technically was working for both Prince John and King Richard) tried to keep control of the region, but succeeded only some of the time. From 1190–91, however, Nottingham fell under the control of Prince John, who brought in his own man, a medieval enforcer called William de Briwere.

De Briwere was one of the most hated and feared men in England and (a rare thing) a favourite of both Richard and John. Richard had appointed him as one of Longchamp's 'supervisors' while he was on Crusade, but Longchamp began to exceed his authority soon after Richard left, and de Briwere quickly shifted his loyalties to John.

De Briwere was everything the stories make the Sheriff out to be – greedy, vain and insanely ambitious. Even the corrupt church hated him, largely because he liked to kidnap the clergy's mistresses and ransom them back again to raise money. In 1210, the people of Dorset and Somerset, where de Briwere was also Sheriff, offered King John a large amount of money to get rid of him. John took the money and simply moved de Briwere to another county to continue his work, which can only have strengthened his terrible reputation.

THE FLYING MONK

In the annals of flight, many are accorded the accolade of 'first man to fly' – the Wright Brothers, of course, and Sir George Cayley, who built the first glider, not to mention the Montgolfier Brothers and their hot-air balloon of 1783.

But there is another claimant for this title, a young Englishman called Eilmer, who allegedly first flew 700 years before the Montgolfiers – in 1010. Eilmer was a monk in the ancient Wiltshire town of Malmesbury. According to the famous local historian William of Malmesbury, who was writing just after Eilmer's lifetime, the monk fastened wings to his hands and feet, launched himself off a tower, probably that of the old Abbey, and flew 200 feet before coming to earth with a bump, breaking both his legs. But this was no impromptu escapade – Eilmer had been studying the jackdaws that lived around the abbey, and had worked out how they used the air currents to glide. On recovering from his first failure, he began planning a second attempt, this time adding a tail to his wings for stability. Sadly the abbot decided enough was enough, and Eilmer's flying days were over.

It is quite possible that what Eilmer had invented was the hang-glider. A stained glass window commemorating his achievement can be seen to this day in Malmesbury Abbey.

PAST PUZZLES

How many drams in an ounce?
Answer on page 145.

OLD PICTURE, NEW CAPTION

Lord Malmesbury demonstrates the time-saving benefits of his new double-ended sideburn trimmer.

STILL LIFE

An oft-repeated story about James, Duke of Monmouth, is that a portrait of his dead body hangs in the National Portrait Gallery, painted after he was executed. The story claims that his head and body were reattached and his portrait was quickly completed before he was reburied. Sadly, the gallery dismisses the story as nonsense, and says that the portrait in question is of an unknown man. But the painting still has a ghoulish secret; it was not uncommon to paint a corpse to preserve the sitter for posterity, and the portrait is almost certainly that of a dead man.

ELEVEN INTERESTING FACTS ABOUT YORK

• The Roman name for York – Eboracum – means 'the place of the yew trees'.

• York is one of the two oldest surviving dukedoms (the other is Gloucester). The title Duke of York was created for Edmund of Langley by his nephew, Richard II.

• York is exactly halfway between London and Edinburgh: about 165 miles each way.

• York Minster is the largest gothic cathedral in northern Europe and took 252 years to build.

• York contains 19 medieval churches.

• The Hansom Cab pub is named after Joseph Hansom, who designed the Patent Safety Cab in 1834.

• The film *Elizabeth*, about the life of Elizabeth I, was the first film to be allowed to use the interior of York Minster as a location.

• York is the most haunted city in Europe, and is home to a whole host of ghosts, including the spirits of a troop of Roman soldiers, which were last seen in 1953.

• York has the longest and best-preserved town walls in England, 3.4km long. They include 45 towers.

• Guy Fawkes was born and educated in York; St Peter's School, which he attended, does not burn a guy on Bonfire Night.

• The Yorkie chocolate bar is made in York (as is the KitKat). York has long been a centre for confectionery, and both Rowntree and Terry's of York began there.

• It is still legal to shoot a Scotsman with a bow and arrow in York, but only within the city walls, and only after dark.

EARLY TRIBAL KINGS

Some of Britain's earliest known, legendary tribal leaders

Beli Mawr, c.100BC, King of Silures and High King,
possibly the father of Lud and Caswallon
Lud/Llud, c.70–60BC, King of Silures, High King,
founder of London
Caswallon, c.60–48BC, King of Cateuvellauni
and High King
Imanuentus, c.55BC, King of Trinovantes, murdered
by Caswallon
Mancubracius, c.54–30BC, King of the Trinovantes,
possibly the grandfather of Boudicca
Cingetorix, c.55BC, one of the tribal leaders of the Cantii
in Kent, led an attack on Caesar's ships off Kentish coast
Commius, c.50–20BC, from Belgic tribe of Atrebates,
forced out of the country; returned as Caesar's agent
but later rebelled against him

MONARCH MNEMONIC

How to remember your kings and queens
Willie, Willie, Harry, Steve
Harry, Dick, John, Harry Three
One, two, three Neds, Richard Two
Harries Four Five Six – then who?
Edwards Four, Five, Dick the Bad
Harries twain and Ned the Lad
Mary, Bessie, James the Vain
Charlie, Charlie, James again
William and Mary, Anna Gloria
Four Georges, William and Victoria
Edward, George, the same again
Elizabeth the Second, and long may she reign!

Britain's worst military disaster took place in January 1842 in Afghanistan. The ruler of Afghanistan, the Amir Dost Mohammed, was so anti-British that Lord Auckland was determined to depose him and substitute Shah Suja, an Afghan noble. Suja was friendly towards the UK and was being kept in India on an allowance for just this purpose. In August 1839, a force of British and Indian troops, grandly called the 'Army of the Indus', invaded Afghanistan and occupied Kandahar, Ghazni and Kabul.

The occupation lasted for 18 months, but after a revolt and the murder of two political agents, it was decided to evacuate the garrisons in the capital. Seven hundred and fifty British and 2250 Indian troops with between 10,000 and 12,000 camp followers left Kabul on 6 January 1842. The weather was abysmal, the ground was covered in snow and the temperature was below freezing. Waiting for them in the mountain passes were the Afghan Ghilzais with their extra-long-barrelled rifles called Jezails. Trained almost from birth, they were reckoned to be the finest marksmen in the world and they had a devastating effect on the long, slow column. The soldiers with their smooth bore muskets stood little chance against them.

It is popularly believed that there was only one survivor of the massacre, a military surgeon called Dr William Bryden, who reached Jellalabad, a fort garrisoned by the Thirteenth, First-Somerset Light Infantry and some native troops. The rest were annihilated by the Afghans or succumbed to the appalling weather. In fact, six other men survived, with a few wives and children, who had been held as hostages in Kabul and were later released. In addition, a few Indian sepoys straggled in later.

LOST HEADS AND HEARTS

The fate of some famous remains:

Anne Boleyn's heart
After she was beheaded on the orders of Henry VIII, Anne's heart was stolen and hidden in a church near Thetford in Suffolk. It was reburied under the church organ in 1836.

Charles I's vertebra
In 1813, the coffin of Charles I was opened and an autopsy performed by royal surgeon Sir Henry Halford. He took a fancy to the king's fourth cervical vertebra and took it home to use at dinner parties as a salt holder. The vertebra was later returned at Queen Victoria's request.

Sir Walter Raleigh's head
After his beheading, Raleigh's wife Elizabeth had his head embalmed and kept it by her side in a leather bag for the rest of her life. Their son Carew kept the head safe until his death in 1666, when it was buried with him and the rest of his father's body. The son, and Raleigh's head, were eventually reburied in West Horsley, Surrey.

Shelley's heart
When romantic poet Percy Bysshe Shelley drowned in Italy in 1822, his body was cremated on the beach. One of his friends, Edward Trelawney, noticed that the heart was not burned, and pulled it from the flames. He gave it to Shelley's friend Leigh Hunt, who gave it to Mary, Shelley's wife. She wrapped it in silk and carried it everywhere, until their son Percy also died, and she buried the heart with him.

THE LIFE OF BYRON

Few of Britain's most famous scoundrels have pursued self-destruction with quite the gusto of George, Lord Byron. Famous for his romantic poetry, Byron himself could not have been less romantic. Born to an unfaithful and profligate father who killed himself, Byron began life badly and continued in the same vein. At Harrow he formed relationships with younger boys, and at university in Cambridge he frequented prostitutes, fell in love with a choirboy and began an affair with a girl called Caroline, whom he liked to dress as a boy. On a tour of Europe he spent much of his time with prostitutes or young men before returning to make his maiden speech in the House of Lords in 1812. The publication of *Childe Harold's Pilgrimage* – the tale of a hedonistic young man – made him famous, and he took full advantage of the female attention that followed. He had a stormy relationship with Lady Caroline Lamb, who coined the phrase 'mad, bad and dangerous to know', but left her to start an affair with his half-sister, who became pregnant. He included the theme of incest in his verse novel *The Bride of Abydos*. He married an heiress, Annabella Milbanke, with whom he committed such unnatural acts that her horrified parents took her back. He was often drunk, bad-tempered and broke, and when London society began to turn its back on him, he left the country after a last fling with Claire Clairmont, who became pregnant. Ensconced in Venice, he kept his house stocked with prostitutes and lovers, including the landlord's wife and a countess named Teresa. But when Teresa left her husband, Byron promptly left her and fled to Greece, where he died of a fever. He was just 37.

The Battle of Rorke's Drift, which took place on 22 and 23 January 1879, is one of history's most stirring conflicts, where victory was achieved in the face of overwhelming odds, thanks to the initiative and sheer courage of the soldiers involved.

When General Lord Chelmsford invaded Zululand, he left behind B Company of the 24th (2nd Warwickshire) Regiment of Foot to guard the Buffalo River crossing at Rorke's Drift. The encampment consisted of a store, a chapel, a temporary hospital and around 150 men.

In command was Lieutenant Gonville Bromhead of the 24th. However, when Prince Dabulamanzikampande ignored the orders of the King and attacked the post with about 4500 Zulus, it was an officer of the Royal Engineers, Lieutenant John Chard, who took command.

Being an engineer, Chard had a good eye for defences and quickly constructed barricades with sacks of corn and an inner barricade made of biscuit boxes. The Zulus attacked head on, wielding their short stabbing assegais, but were unable to reach the men behind the barricades and were blasted by the famous British Infantry rapid rifle-fire, at point blank range. Most of those who did mount the breastwork were killed by the bayonets of the defenders.

After a number of unsuccessful attacks, the Zulus set fire to the hospital by shooting fire arrows into the thatch, trapping the patients, so Private Henry Hook kept the enemy at bay with his bayonet while Private John Williams hacked holes in the mud walls separating one room from another and dragged the patients through one by one.

Fighting went on all night in the fitful glare from the blazing hospital, as the Zulus made charge after charge. One patient,

Corporal Christian Ferdinand Schiess, stabbed three Zulus in quick succession despite being on crutches. In the open air, Surgeon James Reynolds tended to the wounded, despite the life and death struggle going on all around him. Those too badly hurt to shoot reloaded the guns, and resupplied ammunition to those who were still on their feet.

When dawn came at last, the Zulus retreated, taking their wounded with them and leaving about 350 dead in front of the barricades.

Lieutenants Chard and Bromhead were both awarded the Victoria Cross, as were nine others, including Dalton, Hook, Reynolds, Williams and Schiess, the first member of the South African volunteer forces to win a Victoria Cross. The regiment – now the South Wales Borders – has always been proud to claim '11 VCs before breakfast'. In truth the medals were won by eight men from the 2nd Warwickshire, a Royal Engineer, a surgeon from the Army Hospital Corps and a Natal Volunteer.

THE HALF-HOUR WAR

The shortest British war on record took place on 27 August 1896. The British fleet, under the command of Admiral Sir Henry Rawson, turned up in Zanzibar's harbour a couple of days after Sultan Said Khaled had seized power there. The Sultan interpreted the arrival of the fleet as an act of aggression and opened fire on Rawson and his men from his only warship, the *Glasgow*. The considerably larger British fleet promptly fired back, destroying the *Glasgow* and the Sultan's palace and killing 500 of his men. The battle began at 9.12am and lasted 38 minutes.

Boudicca, Queen of the Iceni (died 61AD)

Boudicca was the wife of Prasutagus, the king of the Iceni at the time of the Roman invasion of 43AD. As Prasutagus thrived in the years following the invasion, it is assumed that he had agreed to negotiate with the Romans, as many leaders did, to avoid slavery or annihilation. He bequeathed half his kingdom to the Romans, and the other half to his teenage daughters, an arrangement that Boudicca was content to abide by. However, when the King died, Nero declared the area a slave province, a punishment more usually meted out to those who resisted Roman rule. The Romans began pillaging the kingdom, and when Boudicca protested, she was flogged and her daughters raped. It was a huge mistake on the Romans' part; Boudicca became their worst enemy, and many Britons were so incensed at her treatment that they rose in revolt.

In 61AD the Iceni and the Trinovantes joined forces to destroy first the town of Colchester, a Roman city, and then London. No one was spared; Britons and Romans alike were burned and slaughtered as Boudicca tried to rid the country of both invaders and traitors. The rebels then turned on St Albans, where the Catuvellauni had made peace with the Romans. As battle commenced, it seemed the Britons must win; they vastly outnumbered the Romans and were brave and fierce. But they were also disorganised, which the Romans were not, and the Britons were defeated, with losses of up to 80,000. Boudicca survived, but rather than fall into the hands of the Romans, she took poison and persuaded her daughters to do the same. Although her rebellion failed, she survives in British history as a symbol of courage and patriotism.

FAST FOOD

**Price list from a cookshop in London in 1378,
for ready-to-eat roasted food:**

Heron 18d
Bittern 18d
Pheasant 13d
Capon baked in pastry 8d
Lamb...7d
Baked capon (no pastry).....................................6d
Rabbit 4d
Plover, woodstock, teal.....................................2½d
Thrushes ....2d for 3
Finches...1d for 10

COULD THIS BE AVALON?

Legend has it that Glastonbury Tor in Somerset is the
burial place of King Arthur, the real Isle of Avalon. The
problem with this theory is that, in the story, the Isle
of Avalon keeps appearing and then disappearing, whereas
Glastonbury Tor sticks out like a sore thumb from the
surrounding countryside, and only ever disappears once
a year under a swarm of new age festival-goers.

But it wasn't always so. Until the late eighteenth
century, when the Great Drains began to be built, the
Somerset Levels were tidal, and many hills, including
Glastonbury Tor, were a place of safety until the floods
receded with the tide. And thus, at certain times the 'Island
of Glastonbury' could indeed be said to have appeared
and then disappeared again.

CHURCHILL AND THE ADDISONIAN TERMINATIONS

The writer and politician Joseph Addison is perhaps best known for founding *The Spectator* in 1711, but in his day he was also notorious for ending his sentences with a preposition, a practice to which he was said to be addicted. The classical scholars of the time abhorred the behaviour, insisting that no sentence should end with a preposition. But Addison took no notice and wielded his terminations with impunity. His 'Addisonian terminations' are still frowned upon by grammatical experts, but centuries after his death, Addison found a supporter in Winston Churchill, who, when told that his sentences should not end in prepositions, retorted, firmly: 'This is a situation up with which I will not put.'

THE DUTIES OF A SHERIFF

- To superintend revictualment of the castle
- To provide funds for the siege of the castle
- To expel intruders into manors and to arrest rebels with *posse comitatus* (ie using citizens rather than soldiers)
- To maintain the peace of the realm with *posse comitatus*
- To summon 12 men of the county to attend to justice
- To enquire into the capture of King's officers by rebels
- To enforce observation of the great charter
- To summon complainants to the King's court
- To send revenues of counties, hundreds and demesnes to the King
- To summon tenants in chief, burgesses and knights of the shire before justices of the eyre
- To send knights to confer with the King
- To elect coroners
- To attend the King

Flower of Scotland

O Flower of Scotland,
When will we see your like again
That fought and died for
Your wee bit hill and glen.
And stood against him,
Proud Edward's army,
And sent him homeward
Tae think again.

The hills are bare now,
And autumn leaves lie thick and still
O'er land that is lost now,
Which those so dearly held
That stood against him,
Proud Edward's army
And sent him homeward
Tae think again.

Those days are past now
And in the past they must remain
But we can still rise now
And be the nation again!
That stood against him
Proud Edward's army
And sent him homeward
Tae think again.

O Flower of Scotland,
When will we see your like again
That fought and died for
Your wee bit hill and glen.
And stood against him,
Proud Edward's army,
And sent him homeward
Tae think again.

OLD PICTURE, NEW CAPTION

*Richard the Lionheart's press officer tries out
some ideas for a Crusades recruitment poster.*

MODERATION IN ALL THINGS

When Lionel, Duke of Clarence, married his Italian fiancée
in 1368, her dowry included the truffle hills of Alba.
The white truffles that they yielded were considered to be
an aphrodisiac, and a quantity of them was provided at the
wedding feast. Sadly the Duke partook of so many that
he died of a surfeit before he was able to find out
if they worked.

Clive of India (1725–1774)

Robert Clive was born in Shropshire in 1725. At the age of 18, he obtained a clerkship with the East India Company in Madras, which, two years later, was captured by the French. Clive was taken prisoner but escaped and in 1747 was commissioned as an Ensign in the East India Company's army. He was rapidly promoted after leading the company's troops in several engagements, achieving dazzling victories in every case.

At Arcot, capital of the Carnatic, on 31 August 1755, as a mere Captain, he led 200 men from the first Madras European Regiment and 300 sepoys, and captured and occupied the half-ruined fort. There, he resisted a siege of 50 days and finally beat off the attacking force of 10,000 trained troops of the Nawab and 300 Frenchmen.

His greatest success was at Plassey on the 23 June 1757. With 300 men of the 39th Foot (later the Dorsetshire Regiment – the first English regiment to serve in India) 750 Madras Europeans and 1500 Indian troops, he defeated the 50,000-strong army of the Nawab of Bengal and established British supremacy, as he had done at Arcot in Madras.

However, the climate and strains of combat took their toll and he was invalided home, and found himself a national hero. He made – and spent – a fortune, and returned to India in 1755, where he was appointed Governor of Bengal in 1757. When he returned to England a few years later, he was elected MP for Shrewsbury and created Lord Clive.

In 1765, he went back to India to sort out the corruption and disorder in Bengal, but made many enemies in the process. He was recalled to England to face a parliamentary enquiry, which censured him for his methods. The Commons agreed that he had rendered great service to his country, but he was upset by the damage done to his reputation, and committed suicide in 1774.

FAMOUS LAST WORDS

The parting words of some historic figures:

By the Immortal God, I will not move.
Thomas Love Peacock, writer, who burned to death in 1866 trying to save his beloved library of books.

Oh, I am so bored with it all.
Winston Churchill, prime minister. Died 1965.

When I am dead, I hope it may be said, His sins were scarlet, but his books were read.
Epitaph written for himself by **Hilaire Belloc**, though not inscribed on his tombstone. Died 1953.

I realise that patriotism is not enough. I must have no hatred or bitterness towards anyone.
Edith Cavell, nurse, executed by a German firing squad in 1915.

I am going outside and may be some time.
Captain Lawrence Oates, as he sacrificed his own life in 1912 to save those of his fellow explorers on their ill-fated Antarctic expedition.

So little done. So much to do!
Alexander Graham Bell, inventor of the telephone. Died in 1922.

IT COULD BE YOU

Britain's first National Lottery was launched in 1567 to pay for a variety of public works. The tickets cost 10 shillings each, of which 400,000 were sold and the first prize was £5000, although only £3000 was paid in cash; the rest was paid in a variety of goods, such as cloth, tapestry and plate. It was a one-off event and was very successful, but was not repeated until the following century, and did not become a weekly fixture until over 400 years later.

I PROMISE TO PAY THE BEARER

The oldest surviving printed Bank of England note was made out to... a value of £555, and is dated 1793.

The largest notes printed by the Bank of England... are worth £100 million, but are for accounting purposes only, not for public issue.

The highest denomination note issued for public use... was worth £1000, and was first printed in 1725. It was last issued in 1943 and ceased to be legal tender on 16 April 1945.

The lowest denomination note issued for public use... was for 10 shillings, issued in 1914. It ceased to be legal tender in June 1920.

KINGS IN WAITING

Eldest sons who should have been king but never quite made it

Edward, *son of Edward III* Died 1376, a year before his father.

Edward, *son of Henry VI* Died 1471, as did his father.

Edward, *son of Richard III* Died 1484, a year before his father.

Arthur, *son of Henry VII* Died 1502; his brother Henry suceeded in 1509.

Henry, *son of James I* Died 1612, 13 years before his father; his brother suceeded instead, becoming Charles II.

James, *son of James II* James II was replaced as king by his daughter and son-in-law Mary and William, thus moving the line of succession sideways.

Frederick, *son of George II* Died 1751, nine years before his father; his son became king.

Thomas Hobbes (1588–1679)

Hobbes was allegedly born prematurely, after his mother was startled by news of the approach of the Spanish Armada. Educated at Magdalen Hall, Oxford, he translated some of Francis Bacon's essays into Latin, was mathematics tutor to the Prince of Wales, and met Galileo and Descartes on a tour of the Continent. He believed that the basis of all knowledge was sensation, and that our reactions are always aimed at self-preservation. From this he concluded that man was basically selfish and therefore needed an absolutist government to enforce law and order. This found him no supporters in the church, and unfortunately led the Royalists to believe he supported Cromwell. He also believed that man could be diverted from vice by poetry and he was a master of irony, not least in his work *Leviathan*, in which he compared the papacy to the kingdom of the fairies. A central feature of his philosophy was that the life of man is 'solitary, poore, nasty, brutish and short'.

HISTORIC WORDS

'...bruised beans, two modii, chickens, twenty, a hundred or two hundred eggs, if they are for sale there at a fair price...8 sextarii of fish sauce... a modius of olives.'

A letter to the slave of Verecundus, a prefect at the Roman settlement of Vindolanda, one of the main military posts in the north of Britain before the building of Hadrian's Wall.

The shopping list dates back to around 100AD and is one of the oldest surviving handwritten documents to be found in Britain. It was written on a wafer-thin slice of wood, using carbon ink and a quill-type pen.

TOO MANY COOKS

Between 30 October 1683 and 6 February 1685, there were eight British heads of state and future heads of state alive, the most to be alive simultaneously. They were Charles II, James II, William and Mary, Anne, George I and George II, as well as Richard Cromwell, the second Lord Protector.

THE OTHER PATRON SAINT OF ENGLAND

Edmund, the last king of the East Angles, is one of Britain's forgotten heroes. Around the time of his reign in the ninth century, England was suffering periodic raids by the Vikings, although they usually returned to their homeland to enjoy their spoils. But by 865 they were settling rather than leaving, and were becoming more rapacious and violent. Edmund decided it was time to make a stand. The Danes often negotiated with the local kings, but Edmund refused to concede to their unreasonable demands. In 869, a battle was fought at Hellesdon, at which Edmund was captured and executed. Reports vary as to how he was killed; some say that he was shot to death with a great quantity of arrows, others that he was flayed, tortured and beheaded, after which soldiers found a wolf standing guard over his severed head. When his body was reburied in 915, it was found to have suffered very little decay, and Edmund began to attract a cult. Within a few decades, he was regarded as one of England's patron saints, until his memory was displaced by St George. But Edmund's name lives on in the town where he was reburied, formerly known as Bedricsworth. In the fine tradition of calling a spade a spade, it was renamed Bury St Edmunds.

OLD PICTURE, NEW CAPTION

*'What do you mean, the train hasn't been invented yet?
I've got a meeting in Guildford in an hour.'*

LONELY HEARTS CLUB

When a spinster named Helen Morison became the first
person in Britain to advertise for a husband, by placing
a notice in the *Manchester Weekly Journal* in 1727,
there was such outrage at her immorality that
the Lord Mayor had Miss Morison committed to
a lunatic asylum for four weeks.

TWENTIETH-CENTURY CRISES

The Suez Crisis (1956)

In 1956, the Suez Canal Company was largely controlled by the British government, and the canal itself was of huge strategic importance. The French had the next biggest stake. An agreement signed in 1888 gave the Suez Canal Company concessionary rights to the use of the canal until 1968. However, in July 1956, President Nassar of Egypt nationalised the Canal Company, in order to use the shipping tolls to build the Aswan High Dam. The British government, led by Anthony Eden, secretly resolved to bring down the Egyptian government, and the British, French and Israeli governments hatched a plan in which Israel would attack Egypt, and the British and French would come in to mediate and regain control of the canal. The Israeli invasion went ahead on 29 October, followed by the British and French landing on 5 November, which set off an international uproar. All three countries were forced to withdraw and were replaced by a UN peace-keeping force. Anthony Eden resigned in January 1957 on the grounds of ill-health.

SHORTEST PEERAGE

The shortest peerage in Britain lasted a split second, due to a legal technicality. The law assumed that the Hon Wilfrid Carlyl Stamp, the second Baron Stamp, survived his father by a split second on 16 April 1941, when he and the first Baron Stamp were both killed in an air raid.

The shortest recorded peerage apart from this unlikely event was that of 30 minutes; 13-year-old Charles Brandon, third Duke of Suffolk, died 30 minutes after succeeding his elder brother, Henry, when both were felled by a fatal illness on 14 July 1551.

NINE TO FIVE

The alternative careers of some historic figures

Joseph Addison, *writer* . . . . MP for Malmesbury
Clement Attlee, *prime minister* . . . . social worker
Alexander Graham Bell, *inventor.* .speech teacher to the deaf
Arnold Bennett, *writer* . . . . solicitor's clerk
Daniel Defoe, *writer* . . . . brickmaker and shopkeeper
Benjamin Disraeli, *prime minister* . . . . novelist
John Donne, *poet* . . . . Dean of St Paul's
Michael Faraday, *scientist.* . . . . bookseller
and laboratory bottle-washer
Edward Gibbon, *historian* . . . . MP for Liskeard
Gerard Manley Hopkins, *poet* . . . . classics professor
Harold Macmillan, *prime minister* . . . . publisher
Isaac Newton, *scientist* . . . . Master of the Royal Mint
and Member for Parliament
George Orwell, *writer* . . . . policeman
Walter Raleigh, *explorer* . . . . MP for Devon
Laurence Sterne, *writer* . . . . vicar
Edmund Hillary, *mountaineer* . . . . beekeeper

THE ENDLESS PARLIAMENT

The longest English parliament... lasted for 17 years, eight months and 16 days. It was known as the 'Pensioners' Parliament' and took place during the reign of Charles II, from 8 May 1661 to 24 January 1679.

The longest United Kingdom parliament... was during the reign of George V, Edward VIII and George VI, lasting an unbroken nine years, six months and 20 days, from 26 November 1935 to 15 June 1945.

The shortest parliament... was that of Edward I, which lasted only one day, 30 May 1306.

MURDERED MONARCHS

Edmund I Killed during a fight at a feast in 946.

Duff of Scotland Killed in 954 in Moray.

Edward the Martyr Killed in 978 by supporters of his younger half-brother, Ethelred.

Edmund II, 'Ironside' Killed in 1016, probably by supporters of Canute.

Malcolm III of Scotland Ambushed in 1093 by the Earl of Northumberland.

William II Killed in 1100 by an arrow, while out hunting.

Edward II Killed in Berkeley Castle in 1327, on the orders of his wife Isabella and her lover.

Richard II Killed at Pontefract Castle in 1400 after being deposed by Henry IV in 1399.

James I (Scotland) Killed by assassins in 1437.

Henry VI Killed in 1471 at prayer in the Tower of London, possibly by the future Richard III.

Edward V Murdered in 1483 at the age of 12, probably on the orders of Richard III.

James III (Scotland) Killed in 1488, after the royal army was defeated at Sauchieburn.

Lady Jane Grey Executed in 1553 after nine days as queen.

Charles I Tried and executed in 1649.

GREAT BRITISH FIRSTS

1809 Britain's first letter box is installed in Wakefield, set into the wall of a post office.

1814 The UK's first art gallery opens, the Dulwich College Picture Gallery in London.

1825 A blood transfusion saves a life for the first time in the UK.

1832 The first book in the world to have a book jacket, *The Keepsake*, is published by Longman.

1840 The GPO issues the world's first official prepaid adhesive postage stamp, the Penny Black.

1843 Britain's first garden gnome is imported from Nuremberg by Sir Charles Isham of Lamport Hall, Northants.

1846 Ether is used as an anaesthetic for the first time in the UK, on 19 December, for a dental extraction.

1850 Elizabeth Blackwell becomes the first woman to be recognised in the UK as a qualified physician, after gaining her qualifications in America.

1851 Crystal Palace becomes the first large prefabricated building in the world.

1852 The UK's first pillarboxes are installed in Jersey, at the instigation of writer Anthony Trollope.

1863 The first underground railway in the UK opens, the Metropolitan Line from Paddington to Farringdon.

1865 Elizabeth Garrett Anderson becomes the first woman to qualify as a doctor in the UK.

OLD PICTURE, NEW CAPTION

Centuries before Saddam Hussein employs look-alikes as protection against his enemies, Richard III has the same idea.

THE INFLUENZA PANDEMIC

The most severe epidemic to hit the UK in the twentieth century was an outbreak of influenza, which began in 1918. The Spanish flu, as it was called, swept across the world, killing young and old, strong and weak alike. The US and India suffered the highest mortality rates, and the healthy seemed to succumb to the illness more quickly than the weak, putting paid to the suggestion that it spread because its victims had been weakened by the deprivations of World War One. The outbreak killed around 200,000 people in Britain and about 10,000 British servicemen.

THE FIRST BRITISH PRIME MINISTERS

1721 .... Sir Robert Walpole
1742 .... Earl of Wilmington
1743 .... Henry Pelham
1754 .... Duke of Newcastle
1756 .... Duke of Devonshire
1757 .... Duke of Newcastle
1762 .... Earl of Bute
1763 .... George Grenville
1765 .... Marquis of Rockingham
1766 .... Earl of Chatham
1768 .... Duke of Grafton
1770 .... Lord North

PAST PUZZLES

Who was 'The man who lies down to shoot', 'He of the big hat' and 'The wolf who never sleeps?'
Answer on page 145.

Coinneach Odhar

Coinneach Odhar, a one-eyed Scotsman, lived in the Hebrides in the seventeenth century, and was known for his predictions of the future, earning himself the nickname 'The Brahan Seer'. Odhar would stare through a hole in a pebble with his good eye and claim to 'see' the future. He foresaw the invention of the train, the construction of the Caledonian Canal in 1822, the invention of gas lighting and piped water and the Battle of Culloden. 'The bleak moor shall, ere many generations have passed away, be stained with the best blood of the Highlands,' he claimed. 'Glad am I that I will not see that day, for it will be a fearful period, heads will be lopped off by the score, and no mercy will be shown or quarter given on either side.' The battle, in 1746, was indeed ferocious and bloody, with thousands of Scotsmen killed. Odhar later sealed his own fate by telling his employer, Lady Seaforth, that her husband was dallying with another woman overseas; furious, she condemned him to a horrible death, but not before he made his last prediction, which foresaw the end of the Seaforth line. He predicted that a deaf and dumb man would be predeceased by all his four sons and the estate would pass to a woman, who would kill her sister. All of it came true; when the last Seaforth died in 1815, after his four sons, the estate passed to the eldest daughter, who accidentally killed her sister in 1823 while driving a carriage.

PAST PUZZLES

What connects journalist and former MP Martin Bell with *The Times* crossword puzzle?
Answer on page 145.

THE ORIGIN OF SURNAMES

Surnames first came into use in England in the twelfth century, because of a growth in population after the Norman Conquest and the difficulty of identifying people correctly in the Domesday Book. In Wales, surnames did not appear much until the early seventeenth century, due to the tradition of oral pedigrees being handed down by the Bards.

The origin of a surname falls into one of five categories:

Patronymic This indicates a relationship. For example, Johnson, John or Johns mean 'son of John', and Dickinson means 'son of Richard'. Sometimes forenames simply became surnames without the 'son', such as James or Paul. Scottish names beginning with Mc come into this category: McDougal is 'son of Dougal'. The Irish prefix O' does the same job. Welsh patronymic names stem from the Welsh 'ap' or 'ab' meaning 'son of', from which we get Pugh (ap Hugh, son of Hugh), Price (ap Rhys) and Bunyan (ap Onion) and Bowen (ab Owen).

Locative These names – such as the classic Norman 'de' – show where a man lived or came from, or in some cases that he owned that place. The 'de' was later dropped from many names, leaving just the place name itself. So names such as Kent, Derbyshire, Devonshire and Lancashire indicate a place of origin.

Topographical Describes the place of residence. Many are obvious: Tower, Field, Fieldhouse, Hill, Churchman, Cross, Ridge, Shaw, Marsh, Atwell, Green and Wood. More unusual are Holt (a wood), Combe (tree-covered hill), Kerr or Carr (marshy ground) and Yeo (West Country for brook).

Occupational These are easily recognised: Weaver,

Tailor, Baker, Miller, Turner, Clerk, Carpenter, Dyer and the ubiquitous Smith are all self-explanatory. There were also blacksmiths, whitesmiths, goldsmiths, silversmiths, locksmiths, greensmiths (coppersmiths), knifesmiths (from which comes Naismith) and tinsmiths. Some are not quite so obvious – for example, Fletcher for a maker of arrows, Telford for a maker of iron and Tranter for a carrier. Surnames are also derived from offices held, such as Knight, Squire, Burgess, Yeoman, Freeman, Bishop, Lord and Abbot.

Nicknames Short, Long, Round, Small, Little and Large indicate physical stature, while Black, Grey, White and Reed (red) describe colourings, as do Fairfax and Blundell for blondes. Ballard was a bald man and Giffard had fat cheeks; Cripps was curly-haired and Hoare was hoary or grey. Spelling, of course, has always been as the writer heard the name, so Reed is the same as Read and Rede, and Clerk and Clark are interchangeable, as are Taylor and Tailor, Shepherd and Sheppard and so on.

THE SEVEN KINGDOMS OF BRITAIN

When Britain was settled by the Angles, Saxons and Jutes after the Romans left, it comprised the following kingdoms:

East Anglia • Essex • Kent • Mercia
Northumbria • Sussex • Wessex

GOOD IDEAS

The first five patents awarded in Britain

Engraving and printing the King's head on documents
Nicholas Hillyard *5 May 1617*

Locks, mills and other river and canal improvements
John Gason *1 July 1617*

Oil for suits of armour
John Miller and John Jasper Wolfen *3 Nov 1617*

Tunnels and pumps
Robert Crumpe *9 January 1618*

Making maps of English cities
Aaron Rathburne and Roger Burges *11 March 1618*

These were the patents awarded when the system was first formalised, although it could be argued that the very first patent was awarded in 1449 by Henry VI to John of Utyman for making the coloured glass for the windows of Eton College

THOSE WHOM THE GODS LOVE...

Creative spirits who died too young

Thomas Chatterton, *poet*	17
John Keats, *poet*	25
Aubrey Beardsley, *artist*	25
Percy Bysshe Shelley, *poet*	29
Wilfred Owen, *poet*	25
Rupert Brooke, *poet*	27
Anne Brontë, *novelist*	29
Christopher Marlowe, *playwright*	29

George II will perhaps go down in history as one of England's most bad-tempered kings. Inheriting the throne from his father, George I, who had been reluctant to leave his native Germany, George II set about outgrumping the father he detested. Once on the throne, George brought dullness to his court, insisting on perfect etiquette and punctuality at all times. He would hold long, boring monologues on his own military exploits, his favourite subject after the state of the economy.

George, like his own father, hated his eldest son, Frederick. 'Our first-born is the greatest ass, the greatest liar, the greatest canaille and the greatest beast in the whole world and we heartily wish he was out of it,' harrumphed the King (although some claim these to be the Queen's words). Described by his son as having an insatiable sexual appetite, George II took a German mistress, whom he commanded his wife to like.

When Queen Caroline began to die a lingering death, the King merely asked her how she expected him to sleep when she would not lie still (although he admitted to being upset when she did die). But George just got grumpier. 'I am sick to death of all this foolish stuff and wish with all my heart that the devil may take all your bishops, and the devil take your Minister, and the devil take your parliament and the devil take the whole island provided I can get out of it and go to Hanover,' he declared.

George's reputation was saved by war: at the age of 60, he fought alongside his troops against the French at Dettingen in 1743. This boosted his popularity, and he took advantage of this to make a visit to his beloved Hanover, a trip that became so lengthy that he had to be persuaded to come home. His reputation was to suffer one final indignity: George II died of a heart attack while sitting on the lavatory.

GREAT BRITISH FIRSTS

1495 The first dry dock in the world opens in Portsmouth.

1604 The first English dictionary is published, entitled *A Table Alphabeticall* by Robert Cawdrey.

1704 The first alphabetical encyclopedia in the world is published, *Lexicon technicum*, edited by John Harris.

1738 A local midwife in Charlemont, Ireland performs the first Caesarian on record in the UK; mother and child survive.

1744 The first golf club in the world opens, The Honourable Company of Edinburgh Golfers.

1769 Honoretta Pratt is the first person to be cremated in the UK.

1777 The first boat in the world to have an iron hull is built in Yorkshire.

1779 The world's first iron bridge, designed by Abraham Darby III, is completed in Shropshire.

1794 A house in Redruth, Cornwall is the first to be lit by gas, which is piped in from an enclosed coal fire.

PAST PUZZLES

Why would huffcap, mad dog, angel's food
and dragon's milk be bad for you?
Answer on page 145.

STRANGE CUSTOMS

Weighing the Mayor

Every year in High Wycombe, a mayor is elected. But before he or she can take office, they have to be weighed – in public. The tradition is unique to High Wycombe and was thought to date back to a pointed remark made by Queen Elizabeth I about the size of the town's dignitaries. However, records of the actual ceremony date back only to Victorian times. The unfortunate mayor sits on a flimsy chair suspended from an equally flimsy looking tripod, underneath a dial that reveals his or her weight. In the spirit of fairness, the charter trustees, honorary burgesses and outgoing mayor are also weighed. To add insult to injury, the Macebearer shouts out the weight for all to hear, adding 'and some more' if they have gained weight since last year. Jeers and whistles duly accompany any extra poundage, to protest that the undignified dignitary has grown fat at the townspeople's expense. A weight loss, on the other hand, is greeted with applause, as the mayor has clearly been working him or herself to the bone.

BRITAIN'S FIRST PUBLIC SCHOOLS

Name of school	Founded
King's School, Canterbury, Kent	597
King's School, Rochester, Kent	604
St Peter's, York	627
St Alban's	948
King's School, Ely	970
Norwich School	1096
High School of Glasgow	1124
Westminster	1179
High School of Dundee	1239
Royal Grammar School, Worcester	1291

The editorial committee agreed that they should publish Shakespeare's first play, but his suggested title of 'Whoops, There Go My Pantaloons' would need some work.

BRITAIN'S FIRST UNIVERSITIES

University	Founded
Oxford	1249
Cambridge	1284
St Andrew's	1411
Glasgow	1451
Aberdeen	1495
Edinburgh	1583
UMIST	1824
Durham	1832
London	1836
Manchester	1851

LESSER-KNOWN BRITISH ECCENTRICS

William Beckford (1760–1844)

William Beckford, heir to his wealthy father's Wiltshire estate, showed great intellectual promise from an early age, taking music lessons from Mozart, learning Persian and writing Gothic novels. But his promising career was cut short by rumours of a relationship with the 10-year-old Earl of Devon. Beckford became a social outcast and was denied a peerage by George III. He eventually fled the country, supported by his £1 million inheritance.

For 13 years Beckford travelled the continent with his doctor, maître d', baker, cook, valet, three footmen and 24 musicians, who, in turn had to transport his bed, cutlery and crockery, books and prints. During a stay in Portugal, Beckford imported a flock of sheep to make the view from his window more like home.

He eventually tired of this itinerant life and went home, where he concentrated all his energies on the building of Fonthill Abbey, which included a 300-foot octagonal tower. He supplied the builders with alcohol to ensure that they worked through the night, seven days a week, with the consequence that the tower fell down three times during its construction. Unable to wait, Beckford ordered that Christmas dinner be served in the abbey before the mortar was quite dry, and as the servants carried in the meal, the kitchen collapsed behind them. However, as soon as enough parts of the abbey could be persuaded to stay up, Beckford entertained his few associates, including Lord Nelson. He loved animals and shared his closely guarded home with his dogs: Mrs Fry, Nephew, Tring and Viscount Fartleberry. Forced to sell the abbey in 1822, Beckford moved to Bath where he constructed another tower, this time a mere 120 feet high. The tower is now a museum dedicated to his memory. The Fonthill tower, however, did not stay the course – it fell down for the last time in 1825.

The earliest trace of human habitation in Britain was found at Boxgrove, near Chichester. The site was the camp of a group of Paleolithic hunters, and the bones were of an early species of human, *Homo heidelbergensis*, dating back 500,000 years. This is the earliest inhabitant of these islands that historians have so far been able to identify. At that time, so much of the world's water was frozen that sea level was 100 metres or more lower than it is today. Britain was joined to what is now Europe, and the first inhabitants of the British Isles probably arrived here on foot.

Over the last 700,000 years, the climate in Britain and elsewhere has gone through a process of alternating glaciation and warming; the last glaciation, or Ice Age, occurred around 13,000 years ago. It is assumed that humans came and went during this time, as the weather dictated, and that the fully modern ancestors of man,

Homo sapiens, arrived here 30,000–40,000 years ago. A fragment of a jawbone was found in Kent's Cavern in Devon, belonging to one of these early humans. But the population only really began to grow and spread when the Mesolithic, or Middle Stone Age, period began in 10,000BC. Then, as the ice melted, the waters rose and Britain was cut off from the continent for good some time around 7000BC. Fortunately for these early Britons, in 8000BC or thereabouts the climate in Britain had improved rapidly, and the island has been inhabited more or less continuously ever since.

This early Britain was probably covered with huge forests, and the hunter-gatherers who lived here would have relied on wild food, including meat – deer and wild pig – wild plants and fruit. Remains of stone axes and bows and arrows show that they perfected their hunting skills. As time passed, those living near the coast learned to enjoy seafood, while those living in areas of sandy soil created clearings that encouraged animals to gather and graze. New arrivals from the continent around 4000–3000BC – the beginning of the Neolithic era – brought domesticated animals as well as the technique of growing crops and of making pottery. By 3000BC Britain was becoming a nation of farmers. The inhabitants began to build; tombs, enclosures and mon- uments began to shape the landscape, many of which are still standing, and towards the end of the Neolithic era more and more people were creating settlements, instead of moving around the country with the seasons. The Britons also discovered that stone and precious metals were buried in the land, and mining brought forth copper, flint, tin and iron, as well as precious stones for ornaments. Man had taken control of the land – and civilisation had begun.

HISTORY REPEATS ITSELF

On 10 November 1918, the Armistice ending World War One was signed by representatives of Germany and the Allied forces in a railway carriage at Compiègne in France, 40 miles outside Paris. On 22 June 1940, Adolf Hitler insisted that French representatives sign an armistice with Germany in the same railway carriage, parked at the same spot.

GLOBAL WARMING

The hottest day on record in the UK was 10 August 2003, when the temperature reached 38°.1C (100.6°F), in Gravesend, Kent.

THE END OF THE PEER SHOW

Lawrence Shirley, the fourth Earl Ferrers, was the last British peer to be executed, and was hanged rather than beheaded, the latter being the usual punishment for a nobleman. Renowned for his foul temper and violent behaviour, Ferrers shot dead his steward after a misunderstanding, and was arrested the next day. He was tried in the House of Lords, where he vigorously defended himself by claiming to be insane (some said there was insanity in the family). However, when the Lords dismissed this as a poor excuse, he heartily agreed and said his friends had put him up to it. He was duly sentenced to death by hanging. The public were agog, and the route to the gallows was so crowded with spectators that it took Ferrers three hours to get there from the Tower, not least because he brought a huge retinue with him, including a cavalry escort. He gave the traditional tip to the executioner's assistant by mistake, and had to wait while the executioner tussled with the assistant to retrieve his fee. When the Earl finally met his end, the fall failed to kill him, and the hapless assistant was forced to pull on his feet to complete the task.

THE NEW BOY

Britain's youngest bishop was Prince Frederick, Duke of York and Albany and the second son of George III, who was elected Prince-Bishop of Osnabrück on 27 February 1764, at the age of six months (196 days). He resigned 39 years later.

THE FIRST CHEMICAL WEAPON

The great secret weapon of the Middle Ages was known as Greek Fire, a stream of flaming oil that, like modern napalm, burned furiously on contact and could not be put out. First used by the Byzantines in the seventh century, the recipe was a very closely guarded secret – so closely that, after a while, even the Byzantines forgot how to make it. The secret, however, was probably not in the mixture itself, but in its delivery. According to medieval sources, the highly potent mixture was pressurised in a large metal container, and then shot out at the enemy like a flamethrower. But although the Byzantine recipe was lost, a form of Greek Fire was successfully used by the Arabs until the early medieval period.

Its first recorded use on British soil was at King Richard's siege of Nottingham Castle in 1194, his first act on returning from Crusade. History assumes that he brought the deadly weapon with him from his encounters with the Muslim armies, particularly at the siege of Acre, at which it was rained down with great effect on the Christian armies. However, the besiegers of Nottingham had been using it since the beginning of the attack, and Richard and his men didn't get there until two days later. So we cannot be sure whose idea it really was – unless bad news travels fast.

FAMILY HISTORY

The last surviving person in Britain whose parents were born in the eighteenth century was Alice Grigg of Kent, who died in April 1970. Her father, William, was born on 26 October 1799.

POPULATION OF WALES

43AD	250,000 (Roman invasion of Britain)
1190	160,000
1290	300,000
1400	200,000 (after the Plague)
1536	278,000
1620	360,000–400,000
1770	500,000
1851	1,163,000
1914	2,523,500
1925	2,736,800
1939	2,487,000
1971	2,731,000
2001	2,938,000

THE ORIGINS OF ALBION

Of the many names that Britain has enjoyed, 'Albion' is perhaps the most romantic. *The Oxford Companion to the English Language* explains that the word probably has a shared Celtic and Latin root, meaning 'white' or 'the white land', possibly referring to the cliffs of Dover that would greet new arrivals. Others suggest that it means 'the world' or simply 'the land'. It has also been suggested that Albion comes from the name of a giant (a son of the sea god, Neptune), from England's first Christian martyr (Alban), or from Princess Albia, the oldest of the 50 daughters of the King of Syria who settled in Britain. Albion was misappropriated in 1793 by Marquis de Ximenes, who first used the words 'perfidious Albion' in a poem, a phrase that was seized upon and re-used in the Napoleonic recruiting drive of 1813.

While working as a waitress at Alexandra Palace in London, 16-year-old Dolly Shepherd stepped from the audience at *Buffalo Bill's Wild West Show* to take the place of his wife, who had been injured during a display of blindfold shooting. In return, Samuel Cody (Bill's real name) introduced her to parachuting.

Dolly – whose real name was Elizabeth – made her first jump at the age of 17, after just 30 minutes of instruction and thereafter took it up as a career, taking part in demonstrations as part of a team. On 9 June 1908, Dolly entered the record books by carrying out the world's first mid-air rescue by parachute. The parachute of her fellow jumper, Louie May, became tangled as the girl clung to the trapeze bar suspended below the balloon. Dolly got the girl out of her harness and ordered her to wrap herself around her rescuer as they fell 11,000 feet, using Dolly's single parachute. They both survived the landing, although Dolly was temporarily paralysed by the fall, but was cured by controversial electric shock therapy. Dolly worked as a parachutist for another four years before giving it up and joining the Women's Air Auxiliary Corps as a driver mechanic. She died in 1983 at the age of 96, having seen the first man walk on the moon, an astonishing contrast to her own airborne career. She also flew with the Red Devils a few years before she died. Dolly's daughter, Molly Sedgwick, celebrated her 83rd birthday in 2003 by making a parachute jump with the Red Devils from 13,000 feet. She raised £6224 for charity.

Thomas Paine (1737–1809)

Thomas Paine was the son of a staymaker, who became one of the country's most famous radical writers. Dismissed from his job for demanding a pay increase for himself and his colleagues, he left for America, where he published a number of outspoken pamphlets. One of the best known of his early publications was *Common Sense* (1776), which advocated the separation of America from Britain and sold around 100,000 copies in its first few months. Paine also opposed slavery and was in favour of the emancipation of women. In 1787 he returned to England, where he published his most famous work, *The Rights of Man*. In it he praised the new constitutions of America and France and criticised that of England, and laid out his ideas on tax reform, family allowances, maternity grants and other liberal and farsighted measures. He despised the flowery writing style of his contemporaries, particularly Edmund Burke, and wrote instead in a plain and simple style unusual for the time. 'Mr Burke should recollect that he is writing history, not plays', he sneered. His later pamphlet, *The Age of Reason* (1793), attacked Christianity, which damaged his reputation in England, and effigies of him were burnt in the street. He was tried in absentia for treason, which meant that he could never return. He eventually sailed back to America, where he lived out his last years. When he died in 1809, his bones were retrieved by fellow pamphleteer William Cobbett, who intended to restore Paine's remains to England, but he managed to mislay the bones before completing his task.

COALS TO NEWCASTLE

A few of Britain's bolder exports:

- The Premier Drum Company of Leicester sold four shipments of tom-toms to Nigeria, and shifted a consignment of maracas to South America.
- Permaflex of Stoke-on-Trent sold £50,000 petroleum to the Arabs in the form of lighter fluid.
- Associated Health Foods of Surrey sold 100 tonnes of wholewheat pasta to Italy.
- Eastern Sands and Refractories of Cambridge shipped 1800 tonnes of sand to Abu Dhabi.
- Unilever Export sold 100 cases of Batchelor's Vesta Chow Mein to Hong Kong.
- Bunce Ltd of Wiltshire sold a snow-plough to Dubai.

American merchant Timothy Dexter did once send coals to Newcastle, which happened to arrive just as the city ground to a halt amidst a coal strike. He made a huge profit.

NOT LONG TO REIGN OVER US

Ten monarchs who spent the shortest time on the throne

Lady Jane Grey	9 days
Aelfweard	16 days
Swein Forkbeard	40 days (king but not crowned)
Edward V	2 months 17 days
Edmund Ironside	7 months (king in London only)
Harold II	9 months
Edward VIII	11 months (not crowned, abdicated)
Richard III	2 years 2 months
Edward the Martyr	2 years 9 months
Harold I	3 years

OLD PICTURE, NEW CAPTION

Early trials of the sleeping policeman, as a traffic-calming measure exposed a few basic design flaws.

FIRST BRITISH DAILY NEWSPAPERS

Daily Courant	1702	London
Belfast News Letter	1737	Belfast
The Press and Journal	1748	Aberdeen
The Herald	1783	Glasgow
The Times	1785	London
The Observer	1791	London
The Courier	1816	Dundee
The Scotsman	1817	Edinburgh
The Guardian	1821	London
Evening Standard	1827	London

NOT QUITE WINNIE THE POOH

Before the days of *Noddy and Big Ears* and *Thomas the Tank Engine*, books written for children were intended quite simply to put the fear of God into their young readers. Uncompromising moral tales and lectures were written to teach children the difference between good and evil, and the terrible consequences of the latter. The books' titles left little to the imagination: *A Token for Children, being an Exact Account of the Conversion, Holy and Exemplary Lives, and Joyful Deaths of Several Young Children* by James Janeway (1671) was a typical example. Another was *A Token for the Children of New-England, Or, Some Examples of Children in whom the Fear of God was remarkably Budding, before they dyed, in several parts of New England. Preserved and published for the Encouragement of Piety in other Children*, by Cotton Mather (1700).

Books were sometimes aimed at parents, too, such as *A Family Well Ordered, or An Essay to render Parents and Children Happy in one another*. In this particular volume, the author leaves the young reader in no doubt as to the consequences of their bad behaviour:

'The Heavy Curse of God will fall upon those Children that make Light of their Parents… The Curse of God! The Terriblest Thing that ever was heard of; the First-born of Terribles!…Children, if you break the Fifth Commandment, there is not much likelihood that you will keep the rest…Undutiful Children soon become horrid Creatures, for Unchastity, for Dishonesty, for Lying, and all manner of Abominations…And because these undutiful Children are Wicked overmuch, therefore they Dy before their Time. Children, if by Undutifulness to your Parents you incur the Curse of God, it won't be long before you go down into Obscure Darkness, even into Utter Darkness; God has reserved for you the Blackness of Darkness for ever.'

THE WELSH NATIONAL ANTHEM

Hen Wlad fy Nhadau

Mae hen wlad fy nhadau yn anwyl i mi,
Gwlad beirdd a chantorion, enwogion o fri;
Ei gwrol rhyfelwyr, gwlad garwyr tra mad,
Tros ryddid collasant eu gwaed.

Cytgan (Chorus):
Gwlad, gwlad, pleidiol wyf i'm gwlad,
Tra mor yn fur
I'r bur hoff bau,
O bydded i'r heniaith barhau.
Hen Gymru fynyddig, paradwys y bardd,
Pob dyffryn, pob clogwyn, i'm golwg sydd hardd;
Trwy deimlad gwladgarol, mor swynol yw si
Ei nentydd, afonydd, i fi.

Os treisiodd y gelyn fy ngwlad dan ei droed,
Mae heniaith y Cymry mor fyw ag erioed,
Ni luddiwyd yr awen gan erchyll law brad,
Na thelyn berseiniol fy ngwlad.

[Cytgan]

There are various translations but the most literal one of the first verse and chorus is:

Land of my Fathers
The land of my Fathers is dear to me,
A land of poets and minstrels, famed men.
Her brave warriors, patriots much blessed,
It was for freedom that they lost their blood.

Homeland! I am devoted to my country;
So long as the sea is a wall
to this fair beautiful land,
May the ancient language remain.

It is often sung by English speakers as:

The land of my fathers is dear unto me,
The land of the poets, the land of the free,
Her patriots and heroes, her warriors so brave,
For freedom their life's blood they gave.

Wales! Wales!
Pledged am I to Wales
Whilst seas surround
This land so proud
Oh, long may our old tongue remain.

STRANGE CUSTOMS

Coracle Regatta

Every August in Cilgerran, Cardiganshire, the Coracle Regatta takes place on the River Teifi, where the waters cascade through a spectacular gorge. Fishermen have used coracles to fish in this country for centuries, and the races are a tribute to the enduring usefulness of this peculiar craft. The village of Cilgerran is at the top of a wooded gorge, and the regatta takes place in the shadow of the old Cilgerran castle that overlooks the river. Various races are held, including single-handed, ladies only and 'foreign' coracles – that is, not of the very specific River Teifi type. Members of the countrywide Coracle Society are made welcome, although the Teifi coracles try fiercely not to be out-run on their own territory. The coracles are made from a willow frame bound with hazel wood, covered with calico cotton and waterproofed with hot pitch and linseed oil. They weigh about 30lb and can be carried on the back like a turtle shell. The older coracles were much heavier, giving rise to the Welsh saying 'Llwyth gwr, ei gorwg' – 'A man's load is his coracle'.

WITCHES, PROPHETS AND MYSTIC MEN

Elizabeth Barton

Elizabeth Barton (1506–1534) was a servant-girl who became a national celebrity after a serious illness plunged her into a trance. Through the haze of fever she began to foresee the future, and was quickly taken under the wing of the Church, who considered her prophecies to be messages from heaven. Soon she was being used as propaganda for the Catholic Church and became something of a celebrity. When King Henry VIII tried to divorce his first wife, Catherine, it was the perfect opportunity for the Church to use Elizabeth to condemn his action, as if in a message directly from God. 'If this king does not desist in this impious action, he will die within seven months and his daughter, Mary, will rule in his stead,' Elizabeth proclaimed. Henry took little notice, divorced Catherine and married Anne Boleyn. The country held its breath. When the King failed to expire after seven months, public opinion turned against Elizabeth Barton, and the King swiftly had her arrested and hanged for treason.

CELTIC TREASURES

Some of Britain's earliest Celtic treasures in the British Museum

Witham Shield: bronze • Third century BC
River Witham, Lincolnshire

Battersea shield: bronze • Second to forth century BC
River Thames, London

Scabbard ornament: bronze • 200BC
Mill Hill, Deal, Kent

THE DAY CRIPPEN'S HEAD FELL OFF

On 7 June 1931, Britain's largest recorded earthquake struck at Dogger Bank, measuring 6.0 on the Richter scale. The tremors were felt all over Britain and as far away as France, Belgium, Germany, the Netherlands and Norway. The greatest damage was reported down the east coast, including the town of Filey, where a church spire was completely rotated. Minor damage occurred as far south as Suffolk, and a factory roof collapsed in Staines. *The Daily Mail*, whose headline read: 'People thrown from their beds' reported that the country shook from Edinburgh to Bournemouth. It also reported the unexpected casualty of Dr Crippen's waxwork in Madame Tussaud's in London. The head of his effigy was shaken off and landed on the foot of Arthur Devereux, the Kensal Rise murderer, who was displayed next to him. As the *Mail* reported: 'Dr Crippen was left standing in his replica of the Old Bailey dock with half a moustache on one shoulder and his spectacles dangling from the other.' Several other waxworks were damaged, including that of tennis player Helen Wills Moody, who lost her right arm. The only real person reported dead was a woman in Hull who died of a heart attack, allegedly brought on by the shock.

PAST PUZZLES

What do King Canute and Jane Austen have in common?
Answer on page 145.

William Caxton, the father of the British printing industry, set a good example by censoring his own publications, replacing 'arse' with 'buttocks' for example, in his translation of Malory's *Le Morte d'Arthur* in 1485. But others were less willing to follow his example and the authorities soon felt compelled to step in.

Henry VIII issued a list of banned books in 1529, including Thomas More's *Utopia*. He also prevented the importing of books written in English, in particular the translations of the Bible by William Tyndale and Miles Coverdale.

In 1557, the Catholic Church began its *Index Librorum Prohibitorum*, in which it listed works that it had censored. The list was frequently republished and at its height listed 5000 banned books, including works by Samuel Richardson and Daniel Defoe.

Elizabethan authorities forbade 'obscenities' on stage, and decreed that plays could not include 'matters of religion or of the governance of the estate of the common weale'. Among others, satirist and playwright Ben Jonson and his cast were sent to jail for performing *The Isle of Dogs* (1597) and *Eastward Ho!* (1605).

Throughout the seventeenth century, the producers of unlicensed publications risked having their ears cropped, noses slit and cheeks branded with the letters S and L ('seditious libeller').

The Civil War saw such severe restrictions placed upon the press that the poet Milton felt compelled to write *Areopagitica* in 1644, protesting against censorship and calling for greater freedom of the press.

The direct political attacks by novelist Henry Fielding – then the manager of the

New Theatre in London – on the royal family and the government in 1737 led to the Licensing Act of the same year, which gave the Lord Chamberlain unprecedented power to suppress theatrical works. Theatrical censorship by the Lord Chamberlain was not abolished until 1968.

Editor Thomas Bowdler produced an edition of Shakespeare's plays in 1818 with all the supposedly rude bits cut out, which gave rise to the term 'to bowdlerise'.

In 1960, the Crown prosecuted Penguin Books for publishing the unexpurgated version of *Lady Chatterley's Lover*. The publisher's acquittal was seen by many as a blow to the Establishment.

STRANGE CUSTOMS

Whuppity Stourie

In Lanark in Strathclyde every 1 March, a group of children run 'sunwise' around the parish kirk, whirling paper balls on string around their heads and beating each other with them as they run in a ceremony known as Whuppity Stourie. They are accompanied by the church bells, which are silent from October to February, but begin ringing again on 1 March. The first boy and girl to complete three circuits win a cash prize, and the rest have to scramble for coins scattered on the ground by the provost. Until the 1900s, the race was more boisterous; young men sped around the church, whirling their caps, then set off for a fight with the lads of Lanark. But the town magistrates banned this version of the ceremony and replaced it with something more innocent. The tradition is thought to have originated in the whipping of penitents around the church, or was perhaps a ritual to exorcise evil spirits, who travel in clouds of dust (stour). In Scottish folklore, Whuppity Stourie is the name of a bad fairy, who is defeated only if her victim can guess her name.

THE BATTLE THAT NEVER WAS

On 24 February 1797, a small French force of three ships of war and a lugger anchored in a small roadstead near Fishguard and proceed to disembark troops. Lord Cawdor, the local militia officer, in his report later said that, on hearing the news, he proceeded to the spot with a detachment of the Cardigan Militia and 'all the provincial forces he could collect'. However, he failed to mention in his report the Castle Martin Yeomanry, who got there before him. But Lord Milford, the Lord-Lieutenant of the county, also wrote a report, which said that 'before the troops arrived, many thousands of the peasantry turned out, armed with pikes and scythes, to attack the enemy'. Legend has it that the magnificence of the yeomanry's uniforms convinced the French that they were part of a much larger army, more of whom appeared on the hills overlooking the bay. The 'troops' on the hills were, in fact, a large number of local Welsh ladies, dressed in their tall black hats and red cloaks, marching up and down in a fearsome manner. But the French were deceived, and promptly surrendered.

The yeomanry eventually did get the credit for their prompt turnout and were belatedly awarded their Battle Honour in 1853, the only Battle Honour to be won in Britain.

PAST PUZZLES

What were dredge, maslin, berevechicorn and bollymong used for?
Answer on page 145.

OLD PICTURE, NEW CAPTION

*Lord Melchett hoped no one would notice that
the building costs of his new west wing had been filed
under 'Sundries'.*

WHAT DID THEY DO IN THE WAR?

Kingsley Amis
Officer in Royal Corps of Signals

Tony Benn
Fought against Japan in the RAF

Dirk Bogarde
Captain in the Queen's Royal Regiment; helped to liberate
Belsen

Roald Dahl
Fighter pilot and wing commander in RAF

Denholm Elliott
RAF, shot down and sent to POW camp

Dick Francis
Officer in the RAF

Denis Healey
Beachmaster at the Anzio landings in Italy

Patrick Macnee
Lieutenant in the Royal Navy

Patrick Moore
Navigator in the RAF with Bomber Command

Jon Pertwee
Royal Navy; on leave from his duties when his ship was
sunk by the *Bismarck*

Donald Pleasance
RAF, shot down in France, held in POW camp

Ronald Searle
Captured by Japanese in 1942, worked on Burma-Siam
railway

Peter Sellers
Corporal in RAF

GREAT BRITISH FIRSTS: DRIVING

1862 The first traffic islands in the UK are installed in Liverpool.

1868 The first traffic lights in the UK, semaphore-style signals, are installed off Parliament Square, London.

1896 Bridget Driscoll is knocked down by a car in Crystal Palace, London, and becomes the UK's first traffic fatality.

1896 Walter Arnold becomes the first person to be convicted of speeding in the UK. He drove at 8mph past the house of a policeman in Paddock Wood, Kent, who gave chase on a bicycle and caught him red-handed. He is fined one shilling for breaking the 2mph speed limit.

1903 The first driving licence is issued in the UK for a fee of five shillings.

1903 The first car registration plates introduced in the UK.

1926 The first pedestrian crossing in the UK is installed in Parliament Square, London.

1928 The first automatic traffic lights in the UK are installed for a one-day trial in Wolverhampton (although it was not compulsory to obey them until the 1930 Road Traffic Bill was passed).

1934 Cat's Eyes are first seen on the UK's roads.

1935 The driving test is introduced by Minister for Transport, Leslie Hore-Belisha.

1958 Parking meters are introduced in the UK, in Mayfair, London, on 10 July, costing 6d for one hour.

1960 The first fixed-penalty parking ticket in the UK is issued to Dr Thomas Creighton on 19 September. The £2 fine is waived when it is discovered that he was attending a heart-attack patient.

MUSIC FOR THE MONARCH

Masters of the King's (or Queen's) Music:

1625 Nicholas Lanier
1666 Louis Grabu
1674 Nicholas Staggins
1700 John Eccles
1735 Maurice Greene
1755 William Boyce
1779 John Stanley
1786 William Parsons
1817 William Shield
1834 Christian Kramer
1848 George F Anderson
1870 William George Cusins
1893 Walter Parratt
1924 Edward Elgar
1934 Walford Davies
1942 Arnold Bax
1953 Arthur Bliss
1975 Malcolm Williamson

FEUDAL RANKS

King: Owns all the land, gives away parcels of land (fiefs), in return for future service.

Lords: Hold the land given by the king, which they lease to lesser ranks, who in turn supply the lords with money or knights should the need arise.

Vassals: Pay homage to the lords and lease land to the knights.

Knights: Lease land from vassals, and offer their services in return, when required.

GREAT BRITISH FIRSTS

1919 The first flight out of the UK, London to Paris, costs £21.

1919 The first international airmail from the UK travels from London to Paris.

1921 Marie Stopes opens Britain's first birth-control clinic.

1927 The first transatlantic telephone links open between London and New York.

1932 The first book tokens in the UK are issued.

1945 Family allowance is issued for the first time at a rate of five shillings per child.

1946 The first woman to wear a bikini in the UK is Maisie Dunn, on her honeymoon, on the beach at Newquay.

1946 The first television licence is issued, costing £2.

1954 The first four-minute mile is run by Roger Bannister in Oxford in three minutes 59.4 seconds.

1957 Elizabeth II makes the first sovereign's Christmas speech.

1961 The oral contraceptive is introduced to the UK.

1962 The Brighton Metropole becomes the UK's first legal casino.

1978 The world's first test-tube baby is born in England.

PAST PUZZLES

What do you call a collection of Boy Scouts?
Answer on page 145.

THE WORST STORM IN BRITISH HISTORY

On 14 November 1698, shipowner Henry Winstanley completed the construction of a lighthouse on the treacherous Eddystone rocks, on which he had earlier lost two ships. He took it upon himself to build the lighthouse to prevent further losses, and completed it in spite of being captured by a French privateer halfway through the project. When critics claimed the lighthouse would never survive the winter, Winstanley rashly boasted that his greatest wish was to be safely tucked up in his lighthouse during the worst storm in history.

On 26 November 1703, the east coast of Britain was lashed by weather more severe than had ever before been recorded. It began around midnight, and brought winds so strong that men and animals were lifted from the ground and carried through the air. The roofs were torn from over 100 churches, 15,000 sheep were drowned in floods near Bristol, and 800 houses were destroyed. Ships anchored off the coast were blown against the rocks and each other, and 8000 sailors were drowned in one night. Four hundred windmills were destroyed; some blew over, but others caught fire from the sheer friction of their spinning sails.

Fires broke out in many villages, but the terrified inhabitants were too afraid to leave their homes and brave the storm. They were eventually forced to flee, as the fierce winds fanned the flames and created an inferno. Church steeples and chimney stacks came down everywhere, often killing those who lay or walked underneath.

Much of the devastation occurred in the east of the country, although London suffered too. Every one of the 120 church steeples in the capital was damaged, and trees were ripped from the ground in the city's parks.

As well as the loss of sailors, the storm devastated

the British navy, which lost hundreds of vessels, including four men-of-war. Witnesses reported seeing one ship at Whitstable in Kent being lifted right out of the sea and dropped on dry land. Parliament was particularly concerned at the damage done to its navy, and large numbers of workmen were recruited as quickly as possible to rebuild the country's fleet. Prisoners, including prisoners of war, were offered the chance to redeem their crimes by replacing the many sailors lost in the storm.

As for Henry Winstanley, his wish was granted, although not quite in the way he had envisaged. The day before the storm, he took a party of men out to Eddystone Rocks to make some repairs. By the time the gales had abated, there was nothing left of his wooden lighthouse, or its inhabitants, save for a few pieces of bent iron protruding from the rock.

THE FIRST KNIGHTS OF THE GARTER

King Edward III • Edward (his son), Prince of Wales,
the Black Prince • Henry, Duke of Lancaster
Thomas, Earl of Warwick • Piers de Creilly,
Captal de la Bouch • Ralph, Earl of Stafford
William, Earl of Salisbury • Roger, Earl of March
Sir John Lisle • Sir Bartholomew Burghersh
Sir John Beauchamp • Sir John Mohun
Sir Hugh Courtenay • Sir Thomas Holland
Sir John Grey • Sir Richard Fitz-Simon
Sir Miles Stapleton • Sir Thomas Wale
Sir Hugh Wrottesley • Sir Nele Loring
Sir John Chandos • Sir James Audley
Sir Otho Holland • Sir Henry Eam • Sir Sanchet
Daubrichcourt • Sir Walter Paveley

AGE SHALL NOT WEARY THEM...

Britons who just kept on going:

The Right Reverend Thomas Wilson served as a bishop for 57 years until he died in office in 1755.

Sir Robert Walpole served as Prime Minister for 20 years and 326 days, working into his sixty-sixth year.

Queen Victoria was still on the throne when she died at the age of 81. Her reign lasted 63 years, seven months and three days.

Winston Churchill wrote *A History of the English-speaking Peoples*, aged 82.

William Ewart Gladstone became Prime Minister for the fourth time at the age of 82 and remained PM for two years.

W Somerset Maugham wrote *Points of View*, aged 84.

David Lloyd George, former Prime Minister, remarried, aged 87.

Harry Phillips from Shropshire served as a chorister at his local church from 1893 (aged eight) to 1983 (aged 90).

George Bernard Shaw wrote *Farfetched Fables*, aged 93.

Lord Maenan made his maiden speech in the House of Lords in 1948, at 94 years and 123 days.

PAST PUZZLES

Who was the last English king to die in battle?
Answer on page 145.

THE ANGLO-SAXON CHRONICLE

This early chronicle of Britain is an essential reference for any historian, as it traces the history of the country from the birth of Christ to 1154. It was thought to have been commissioned by the scholarly Alfred the Great, as a way of repairing the damage done to English life by the Vikings, and instilling some sense of his country's history into his subjects. There are seven surviving manuscripts, the last entry for which, in 1154, is the also the last known document to be written in Old English. It brought together the work of Anglo-Saxon monks and priests, including the Venerable Bede, who began writing down their history when Christianity returned to the country in the sixth century. These writings were collected together in the ninth century, and new writings added, up to the mid-twelfth century, as the monasteries carried on the work after Alfred's death. The many different entries range from one-liners to poems and long and lyrical passages, including such stirring stories as the arrival of Hengist and Horsa, and Alfred's last wars against the Danes. It remains a document of enormous historic, linguistic and literary importance.

CELTIC TREASURES

Some of Britain's earliest Celtic treasures in the British Museum

Aylesford bucket: wood and bronze • First century BC
Aylesford, Kent

Two-horned helmet: bronze • First or second century BC
River Thames, London

Mirrors: bronze • First century BC
Desborough, Northamptonshire

OUT OF SIGHT, OUT OF MIND

In 1788, the newly acquired land of Australia became a penal colony for England's criminals. Convicts were taken from the courthouse or the overflowing jails and sent to Australia to serve out their sentence. By 1830, over 50,000 convicts had been sent overseas.

The sentence of deportation was intended for serious crimes such as murder, but it was often misused. The first deportees included a nine-year-old petty thief and an 82-year-old woman accused of perjury. It also didn't take the government long to realise that this was an easy way for them to get rid of people they considered troublesome – such as the Tolpuddle Martyrs. The Martyrs were six lowly paid agricultural labourers from Dorset, who set up a union in Tolpuddle to give their fellow labourers better bargaining power. The authorities were keen to suppress any trade union activity, and the six were falsely accused of taking secret oaths, tried and sentenced to seven years' deportation.

But the authorities had gone too far. The sentence sparked off angry demonstrations and Parliament was forced to issue a pardon, although it was three years before they returned home. Transportation was brought to an end in 1868.

FEUDAL RANKS

Squires: Young knights-in-training, usually aged 14–21.

Seigneurs: Lords of the manor, a manor being the smallest plot of land.

Villeins/serfs: Live on and are bound to a manor or fief. They pay rent to the lord that owns it.

Servants: The lowest in rank. Workers owned by the wealthy, including nobility and wealthy merchants.

TEN DAYS THAT TIME FORGOT

In any historical account of Britain, it can be guaranteed that from 3 to 13 September 1752, absolutely nothing happened – because the days never existed.

At the time, Britain was still using the Julian calendar, a system introduced by Julius Caesar in 45BC. The calendar that had preceded it was complicated and required a group of pontiffs to decide when days should be added or subtracted to keep in harmony with the seasons. Caesar abolished it and replaced it with a year that measured 365.25 days. This meant that a year was 365 days, but every fourth year was 366 days long. He also inserted extra months in the first year of his calendar, which made the year last 445 days, and caused it to be known as the 'last year of confusion'. The first year of this calendar began on 1 January, 46 years before the birth of Christ.

However, this system created an error of one day every 128 years, which, over time, would result in a complete dislocation of dates from their seasons, which became apparent only as the centuries passed. Finally, a physician from Naples called Aloysius Lilius came up with the Gregorian calendar. In this system, a year was 365.2425 days long, and required 97 leap years every 400 years to remain stable. The calendar was anchored by the vernal equinox, which was supposed to take place on 21 March. Because it was by now 1582 and the error of one-in-128-days had been accumulating over the years, the vernal equinox was occurring 10 days early. So 10 days were removed from the year to realign the date.

The Gregorian calendar came into use in 1582, after a papal bill by Pope Gregory XIII. Countries adopting the calendar removed 10 days from their year, 5–14 October. Most of the Catholic countries fell into line, but Britain held out until 1752, by which time it had to remove 11 days from the calendar to keep in step. What should have been 3 September was called 14 September and 3–13 September 1752 were lost for ever.

Sir Francis Bacon (1561–1626)

Educated at Trinity College, Cambridge from the age of 12 or 13, Francis Bacon became a barrister in 1582 and soon after was elected to Parliament. Although not always in favour with Elizabeth I, and often in debt, he prospered, although it was James I who made him a knight, solicitor-general, attorney-general, lord keeper and lord chancellor. However, Bacon's career ended when he pleaded guilty to taking bribes and was effectively cast out of society. He turned to writing and produced a considerable body of work during his life, including *The Advancement of Learning*, in which he classified all the different branches of knowledge, which proved to be a model of secular thought much referred to by later writers. He wrote several more substantial volumes on science and natural history and planned more on philosophy and the intellect, which were never completed. He was a scientist at heart, and believed that it was man's duty to unlock nature's mysteries in order to gain true control over their lives. In a fiercely religious age, he was at heart an empiricist. He wrote a history of Henry VII, which sought to explain, rather than merely chronicle the King's life in the usual manner, and addressed other subjects, including legal principles in *Maxims of the Law* and a series of renowned *Essays*. He died of pneumonia while experimenting with the possibility of freezing food.

PAST PUZZLES

Why was the Korean War bad for British teeth?
Answer on page 145.

GREAT BRITISH FIRSTS: TRAINS AND BUSES

1803 Richard Trevithick builds the first steam locomotive to pull wagons, which ran on the Penydarren Railway in Wales. It was originally built to drive a steam hammer.

1825 The first passenger steam railway opens, running from Stockton to Darlington.

1829 The first scheduled bus service, horse-drawn, runs from Marylebone Road to Bank. The fare was one shilling for the whole journey, 6d for any intermediate stage.

1829 George and Robert Stephenson build The Rocket steam engine, the ancestor of the modern locomotive.

1830 William Huskisson MP becomes the first train accident fatality: he is run down by the Rocket at the opening of the Liverpool and Manchester Railway on 15 September, as he crosses the track without looking both ways.

1831 The first self-propelled omnibus runs from Stratford in London to the City.

1847 The first double-decker bus, built by Adams & Co of Bow, London, takes to the city's streets. Those riding on top were less comfortable, but paid half-fare.

1890 The first electric underground railway in the world opens in London, the City and South London Railway.

1903 The first municipal motor omnibus service in the world is inaugurated on 12 April between Eastbourne railway station and Meads in East Sussex.

1909 The world's first bus conductress is Kate Barton, who worked for her father's bus company in Nottinghamshire.

KITCHEN EQUIPMENT

There should be a provision of good cauldrons to boil large cuts of meat, and a great number of moderate-sized ones for making pottages and for other cooking operations, and great suspended pans for cooking fish and other things and a great number of large and ordinary sized boilers for pottages and other things and a dozen good big mortars...And you will need some twenty large frying pans, a dozen great kettles, fifty pots, sixty two-handled pots, a hundred hampers, a dozen grills, six large graters, a hundred wooden spoons, twenty-five holed spoons, both large and small, six pot-hooks, twenty oven shovels, twenty roasters, both those with turntable spits and those with spits mounted on andirons. You should not put your trust in wooden skewers or spits, because you could spoil all your meat, or even lose it; rather you should have six score iron spits which are strong and thirteen feet long; and you need three dozen other spits which are just as long but not as thick, in order to roast poultry, piglets and water birds...And besides this, four dozen slender skewers for doing glazing and for fastening things.

Instructions for feeding the royal household in 1403

WELL-KNOWN MIDDLE NAMES

Jeremy John Durham [Paddy] Ashdown: *Leader of Liberal Democrat Party, 1988–99*

Nancy Witcher Astor: *First woman MP to take her seat in House of Commons*

Wystan Hugh Auden: *Poet*

Michael Mackintosh Foot: *Leader of Labour Party 1980–83*

LOST VILLAGES

It is estimated that there are more than 3000 'lost villages' in England. The most common reason for their disappearance was the Black Death, when the plague wiped out entire rural populations, and no one wanted to go back for fear of infection. Many were destroyed by war, while in the monastic expansions of the early medieval period, many villages were removed in to make way for a new monastery. In the eighteenth century many super-rich landowners did much the same thing, when looking for the perfect site for their new country estate.

However, many other villages disappeared under more drastic circumstances. Hallsands in Devon was destroyed in 1917 when all but 30 of its cottages were swept away by the sea, while a village under the cliffs at St Ishmael's in Carmarthenshire has been buried under the sand since it disappeared during the great storms of 1606.

Many villages were lost as a result of the building of new reservoirs, among them Derwent and Ashopton in Derbyshire, Mardale in Cumbria, and West End in Yorkshire. Local folklore has it that when the water level is low, the old church tower of West End can still be seen, and its ghostly bell rings out as a lament for the lost village. The same is said of Sutton Bingham in Dorset and Capel Celyn in Wales, as well as other villages 'lost' to the sea, including Shipden in Norfolk and Mabelthorpe in Lincolnshire.

Several villages were not so much lost as stolen, such as Tottington in Norfolk, Imber in Wiltshire and Tyneham in the same county. In all cases, the villages were commandeered by the military during wartime for live-firing practice, with the promise that they would be returned to their owners after the war. They never were.

ENGLISH PLACE-NAMES

Place-names in England largely divide into habitative, such as 'high homestead' or 'long farm', and topographical like 'green hill' and 'clear stream'. There is also a smaller group of names that refers to the settling-place of a particular tribe, usually shown by an –ing ending, such as Hastings, meaning 'Haesta's people'. Below are some common elements of familiar place names around the country:

brough	fortified place (also burgh, bury, borough)
by	farmstead, village
cester	city, town, walled camp (also chester, caster)
fleet	estuary, stream
font	spring (also hunt)
gate	way, road, street (also yate, yatt, yet)
ham	manor, homestead
hay	hedge, fence, enclosed land
hope	dry land in fen, small valley, blind valley
hythe	port, haven (also hive, hithe, eth)
kirk	church
lac	stream, watercourse (also lake, lock, lack)
linch	bank, ridge (also lynch, ling, linge)
mede	meadow (also made, med, meadow)
minster	monastery, church
over	bank, ridge, hill
peth	path, track (also path)
rick	strip of land, narrow road, also ridge
rith	stream (also reth, red)
scough	wood (also skew, scoe)
shaw	copse, grove, small wood
shire	division of the people, division of the kingdom
stowe	holy place, place of assembly (also stoe)
thwaite	meadow, clearing
toft	site of a house, homestead, enclosure
wold	woodland, forest, high forest, open upland
wark	work, fortification

WILLIAM COBBETT AND
THE POTATO PROTEST

William Cobbett (1763 –1835) was a self-educated farmer's son, who became the most famous journalist of his generation, thanks to his refusal to be silenced. After serving as a soldier, he obtained his discharge and retired to France, then to America, where he wrote his first work *The Life and Adventures of Peter Porcupine*, a dangerously pro-British work that did not endear him to the Americans. He returned to England in 1800 and soon shifted from an anti-Radical position to that of Radical. He wrote extensively and forcefully on a wide variety of subjects, and was in favour of such things as universal suffrage and turnips, but very much against Shakespeare, tea and paper money. He was once imprisoned for publishing an attack on flogging in the army, but continued to publish from his prison cell. When an MP referred to his paper as 'two-penny trash', Cobbett obligingly renamed his publication *Cobbett's Twopenny Trash*, which improved his sales figures. He recorded his strong views in exceptional detail, and had a particular hatred for potatoes, which he thought reduced man to the status of a pig. 'Beware of the blasphemous cant of sleekheaded Methodist thieves that would persuade you to live upon potatoes.' He even suggested that the people overthrow the government in order to be free of this wretched vegetable, and protestors did indeed march on Parliament, bearing potatoes stuck on sticks. Cobbett also published a series of essays called *Cobbett's Rural Rides* in which he admired the 'real' countryside and took exception to anything he considered ornamental or fake, such as pruned trees. Despite his prison record and incitement to riot, he was twice elected to Parliament before he died in 1835.

DURING THE COMPILATION OF THIS BOOK, THE COMPANION TEAM...

Reconstructed the Battle of Medway, at which the Britons fought bravely, but the Romans still won

Painted their faces with woad for the staff party

Attempted to name all the British monarchs in order, but kept leaving out King Stephen

Tried to invent something as clever as the traffic light, the tin opener or the concept of parliamentary democracy

Staged a Peasants' Revolt to call for extra bread in the canteen

Set off bravely for the 'North Pole', which would have been an historic expedition had it not been the name of a pub just up the road

Recreated the first glider flight in miniature, using lollysticks, paper, glue and a very long corridor

Failed to agree on whether King Richard I was a Good Man or a Bad King

Wondered how they ever passed their history 'O' Level without knowing the difference between a vassal and a villein

Please note that although every effort has been made to ensure accuracy in this book, the above statistics may be the result of aged and ancient minds.

PAST PUZZLES: THE ANSWERS

P6   The Channel Islands – but he lost the rest of the duchy of Normandy, which at that time belonged to England.

P9   Elvis Presley, aka 'The King' (two hours at Prestwick Airport in Scotland in 1960).

P27   The seven hills of Rome: Capitoline, Quirinal, Viminal, Esquiline, Caelian, Aventine, Palatine.

P46   A way of walking affected by ladies at the court of Queen Alexandra, wife of Edward VII, to make the Queen's own slight limp less noticeable.

P58   Colonel Robert Baden-Powell, so named by the various African tribes whom he met on his travels.

P79   There are 16 drams in an ounce.

P101   His father, Adrian Bell, compiled the first cryptic crossword, in *The Times*, published on 1 February 1930.

P106   They were sixteenth-century, double-strength beers, which the London authorities tried to ban.

P123   Both are buried in Winchester Cathedral.

P126   Cooking; they are all crops grown in medieval England.

P131   A jamboree – the *Oxford English Dictionary* now defines this word as 'a collection of Boy Scouts' after the first mass rally at Olympia in London in 1920.

P134   King Richard III, killed while fighting the forces of Henry Tudor (later Henry VII) at the Battle of Bosworth in 1485.

P138   Hugh Gaitskell imposed charges on dental (and ophthalmic) treatment to contribute to the costs of the Korean War. The remainder of treatments on the recently introduced NHS remained free.

NOTES, THOUGHTS AND JOTTINGS

NOTES, THOUGHTS AND JOTTINGS

NOTES, THOUGHTS AND JOTTINGS

NOTES, THOUGHTS AND JOTTINGS

NOTES, THOUGHTS AND JOTTINGS

NOTES, THOUGHTS AND JOTTINGS

NOTES, THOUGHTS AND JOTTINGS

NOTES, THOUGHTS AND JOTTINGS

NOTES, THOUGHTS AND JOTTINGS

THE HISTORY OF BRITAIN POCKET COMPANION

Jo Swinnerton

PAVILION

A Think Book for Pavilion Books

This edition published by Pavilion Books in 2008
First published in the United Kingdom in 2005 by Robson Books
10 Southcombe Street, London W14 0RA

Imprints of Anova Books Company Ltd

Text and design © Think Publishing 2004
The moral rights of the authors have been asserted

Edited by Jo Swinnerton
The Companion team: Tilly Boulter, James Collins, Rhiannon Guy,
Emma Jones, Lou Millward Tait, Matt Packer, Sonja Patel
and Malcolm Tait

Think Publishing
The Pall Mall Deposit
124–128 Barlby Road, London W10 6BL
www.thinkpublishing.co.uk

ISBN 978-1-862058-22-4

2 4 6 8 10 9 7 5 3 1

Printed and bound by Millenium International Printing, China

The publishers and authors have made every effort to ensure the
accuracy and currency of the information in *The History of Britain
Pocket Companion*. Similarly, every effort has been made to contact
copyright holders. We apologise for any unintentional errors or
omissions. The publisher and authors disclaim any liability, loss, injury
or damage incurred as a consequence, directly or indirectly, of the
use and application of the contents of this book.

www.anovabooks.com

TEENAGE PARENTS

Monarchs who had children exceptionally young

In 1382 **Henry IV and Mary de Bohun** had a son, Edward, when Henry was 15 and Mary was 13. The child died after four days.

In 1457 **Margaret Beaufort** gave birth to a son, the future Henry VII, at the age of 13 years, 7 months and 28 days.

In 1678, Mary, the future **Queen Mary II**, gave birth to a stillborn child at the age of 16. She had two more stillborn children with her husband, William, in the next two years, but the couple never produced a surviving heir.

In 1239 **Eleanor of Provence**, wife of Henry III, gave birth to a son, the future Edward I, at the age of 16.

In 1330, **Edward III** became a father at the age of 17, when his 19-year-old wife, Philippa, gave birth to a son, Edward, the Black Prince.

In 921, **Edgiva**, wife of Edward the Elder, gave birth to a son, the future Edmund I, aged 16.

THE FINAL DROP

The number of hangings in England, Scotland and Wales, in the last 5 years of the death penalty:

1960 – 7
1961 – 4
1962 – 2
1963 – 2
1964 – 2

HABEAS CORPUS

In the late eighteenth century, Scotsman John Aitken had one ambition: to make a name for himself. Having failed to distinguish himself at work, in the army or in America, where he lived for a few years, he set out instead to help America win their war for independence. He planned to do this by the simple expedient of setting fire to all of Britain's shipyards. He managed to set only a few small fires in Portsmouth and Bristol, but it was enough to rattle the authorities. Assuming the arsonist was American, Parliament rushed through a bill that allowed American privateers to be held indefinitely without charges. Their reason was 'it may be inconvenient in many such cases to proceed forthwith to the trial of such criminals, and at the same time of evil example to suffer them to go at large.' This was called the American High Treason Bill, and it caused a number of suspects to be imprisoned without trial in both American and British prisons. However, Aitken was not one of them; when he was eventually caught, he was quickly tried and hanged. The Bill was allowed to lapse when the war was over and Britain's inhabitants regained their right not to be held without trial.

ALL CHANGE

On 9 February 1909, a German military band played 'God Save the King' 16 times in succession on the platform of Rathenau Railway Station in Brandenburg. The lengthy performance was to cover the embarrassment of King Edward VII, who was struggling to get into his Field-Marshal's uniform before emerging.

NOTES, THOUGHTS AND JOTTINGS

NOTES, THOUGHTS AND JOTTINGS

NOTES, THOUGHTS AND JOTTINGS

NOTES, THOUGHTS AND JOTTINGS